28.70

CUR
MID
SOC
LUC
2004

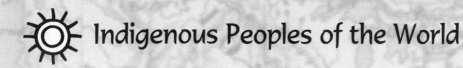

Indonesia

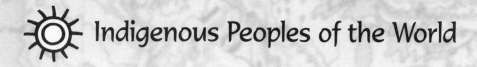

Indonesia

Titles in the Indigenous Peoples of the World series include:

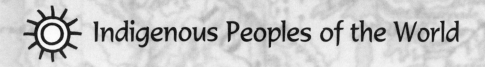

Indigenous Peoples of the World

Indonesia

Mary C. Wilds

LUCENT BOOKS®

THOMSON

GALE

San Diego • Detroit • New York • San Francisco • Cleveland • New Haven, Conn. • Waterville, Maine • London • Munich

© 2004 by Lucent Books. Lucent Books is an imprint of The Gale Group, Inc.,
a division of Thomson Learning, Inc.

Lucent Books™ and Thomson Learning™ are trademarks used herein under license.

For more information, contact
Lucent Books
27500 Drake Rd.
Farmington Hills, MI 48331-3535
Or you can visit our Internet site at http://www.gale.com

LIBRARY OF CONGRESS CATALOGING-IN-PUBLICATION DATA

Wilds, Mary C., 1960–
   Indonesia / by Mary C. Wilds.
      p. cm. — (Indigenous peoples of the world)
Includes bibliographical references and index.
Summary: Discusses the historical origins, beliefs, arts, family life, and future hopes of
the people of Indonesia.
   ISBN 1-59018-314-2 (hardcover : alk. paper)
   1. Indonesia—Juvenile literature. [1. Indonesia.] I. Title. II. Indigenous peoples of the
world (San Diego, Calif.)
   DS615.W554 2004
   959.8—dc22

                                                                              2003012894

Printed in the U.S.A.

Contents

Foreword

Nearly every area of the world has indigenous populations, those people who are descended from the original settlers of a given region, often arriving many millennia ago. Many of these populations exist today despite overwhelming odds against their continuing survival.

Though indigenous populations have come under attack for a variety of reasons, in most cases land lies at the heart of the conflict. The hunger for land has threatened indigenous societies throughout history, whether the aggressor was a neighboring tribe or a foreign culture. The reason for this is simple: For indigenous populations, *way of life* has nearly always depended on the land and its bounty. Indeed, cultures from the Inuit of the frigid Arctic to the Yanomami of the torrid Amazon rain forest have been indelibly shaped by the climate and geography of the regions they inhabit.

As newcomers moved into already settled areas of the world, competition led to tension and violence. When newcomers possessed some important advantage—greater numbers or more powerful weapons—the results were predictable. History is rife with examples of outsiders triumphing over indigenous populations. Anglo-Saxons and Vikings, for instance, moved into eastern Europe and the British Isles at the expense of the indigenous Celts. Europeans traveled south through Africa and into Australia displacing the indigenous Bushmen and Aborigines while other Westerners ventured into the Pacific at the expense of the indigenous Melanesians, Micronesians, and Polynesians. And in North and South America, the colonization of the New World by European powers resulted in the decimation and displacement of numerous Native American groups.

Nevertheless, many indigenous populations retained their identity and managed to survive. Only in the last one hundred years, however, have anthropologists begun to study with any objectivity the hundreds of indigenous societies found throughout the world. And only within the last few decades have these societies been truly appreciated and acknowledged for their richness and complexity. The ability to adapt to and manage their environments is but one marker of the incredible resourcefulness of many indigenous populations. The Inuit, for example, created two distinct modes of travel for getting around the barren, icy region that is their home. The sleek, speedy kayak—with its whalebone frame and sealskin cover—allowed the Inuit to silently skim the waters of the nearby ocean and bays. And the sledge (or dogsled)—

with its caribou hide platform and runners built from whalebone or frozen fish covered with sealskin—made travel over the snow- and ice-covered landscape possible.

The Indigenous Peoples of the World series strives to present a clear and realis- tic picture of the world's many and varied native cultures. The series captures the uniqueness as well as the similarities of indigenous societies by examining family and community life, traditional spirituality and religion, warfare, adaptation to the en- vironment, and interaction with other na- tive and nonnative peoples.

The series also offers perspective on the effects of Western civilization on indige- nous populations as well as a multifaceted view of contemporary life. Many indige- nous societies, for instance, struggle today with poverty, unemployment, racism, poor health, and a lack of educational opportu- nities. Others find themselves embroiled in political instability, civil unrest, and vi- olence. Despite the problems facing these societies, many indigenous populations have regained a sense of pride in them- selves and their heritage. Many also have experienced a resurgence of traditional art and culture as they seek to find a place for themselves in the modern world.

The Indigenous Peoples of the World series offers an in-depth study of different regions of the world and the people who have long inhabited those regions. All books in the series include fully docu- mented primary and secondary source quotations that enliven the text. Sidebars highlight notable events, personalities, and traditions, while annotated bibliogra- phies offer ideas for future research. Nu- merous maps and photographs provide the reader with a pictorial glimpse of each so- ciety.

From the Aborigines of Australia to the various indigenous peoples of the Carib- bean, Europe, South America, Mexico, Asia, and Africa, the series covers a multi- tude of societies and their cultures. Each book stands alone and the series as a col- lection offers valuable comparisons of the past history and future problems of the in- digenous peoples of the world.

"Our Earth and Water"

The indigenous peoples of Indonesia compose a ribbon of cultures, histories, and traditions that stretches across a country at once empty and filled to the brim. They have lived for thousands of years in a region that encompasses more water than land. Indonesia's land mass is a wide sprinkle of more than thirteen thousand islands, many of which were never named. The nation's largest provinces—including Sumatra, Java, Sulawesi, the province of Kalimantan on the island of Borneo, and Papua on the western side of New Guinea—are also its population centers, Java being Indonesia's most crowded island.

Indonesia is home to remarkable animal and plant life, thousands of acres of rain forest, and four hundred active and inactive volcanoes. Its hot, tropical climate and heavy monsoon rains have made it favorable to humans and agriculture since the beginning of human history.

A Girdle of Emeralds

Indonesia's fertile valleys and lush forests made it particularly inviting to human settlement, writes Ailsa Zainu'ddin in her book *A Short History of Indonesia*:

> Indonesia has been called a girdle of emeralds strung around the equator, and green dominates the Indonesian landscape, the somber green of tropical rainforests, the varied greens of coconut palm and banana plant, the brilliant green of young rice in the terraced rice fields.[1]

Yet, she notes, the sea and maritime life have also had a great lure for island peoples. For centuries a thick network of rivers in the interiors of such islands as Sumatra and Java enabled tribesmen to reach the coast via handmade rafts and to bring goods to trade with foreign crews who frequented Indonesia's coast. The monsoon winds that course across Indonesian seas

10

allowed the region's coastal communities to establish busy commercial trade routes that flourished long before European traders arrived.

The sea, too, helped facilitate the human settlement that flowed into Indonesia over thousands of years. Historians believe that a gradual wave of western migrations eventually brought settlers from the Southeast Asia mainland onto the Indonesian islands.

Early Peoples

There is no record of where the very earliest peoples of Indonesia came from, and their culture may have been indigenous to the islands. Very little is known about them, other than that they flourished prior to 3000 B.C. and that they survived by hunting, gathering wild plants, and growing sweet potatoes and yams. Between 3000 and 2000 B.C., a lengthy migration began in southern China and moved across the

Southeast Asian continent. Some of these wanderers stayed in Thailand, Laos, and Cambodia, but others took to the seas in outrigger canoes and eventually settled in Indonesia. Archaeologists believe that this migration was gradual and lasted over thousands of years and that the new arrivals intermarried with the indigenous peoples of the islands.

These mainlanders, they believe, brought rice cultivation and bronze tools with them. A second, smaller group known as the Austronesians settled in Bali and other eastern Indonesian islands. The Austronesians, who began their migration between 2000 and 1000 B.C., were apparently excellent sailors and brought domestic animals, such as water buffalo, pigs, and oxen, to the islands.

Settling an Island Archipelago

The ancestors of these waves of migrants make up the majority of Indonesia's population today. Modern Indonesia is home to hundreds of indigenous groups; the largest of these is the Javanese. This tribe lives in central and eastern Java and constitutes 45 percent of the population. Other tribes include the Sundanese and Madurese, who also live in Java; the Batak, Minangkabau, and Acehnese in Sumatra; the Toraja and Makasserese in Sulawesi; the Dayak peoples of Kalimantan; and the Asmat, Yali, and other peoples of Papua, formerly known as Irian Jaya.

The residents of Indonesia's many smaller islands usually bear the name of their island home; hence, residents of Bali are Balinese, and residents of the Banda island group are Bandanese.

A Life on the Land and Sea

"Indonesians refer to their homeland as Tanah Air Kita (literally 'Our Earth and Water') and the sea has played as important a part in Indonesia's history as has the land,"[2] Zainu'ddin writes. The indigenous peoples did indeed rely almost equally on the land and the sea during their long history. These tribes fished, hunted, farmed, and traded, always attuning their daily lives to the world around them. They did not have the tools to adapt the environment to their needs; thus it was they who adapted to Indonesia's island environment.

Chapter 1

Rice Fields and Spices

When it came to their lifestyles, Indonesia's tribesmen defied easy categorization. Many of them farmed, but those who farmed also fished and kept domestic livestock, and those who hunted also kept livestock and tended gardens of sweet potatoes, taro, and other vegetables as a way to supplement their diets. And those who farmed did not always eat the crops they grew; the Minangkabau, for example, grew vegetables but also grew pepper that was brought to coastal areas and sold to traders who came from as far away as India and China to acquire it. Farmers like the Bandanese devoted most of their agriculture to cash crops: On Banda, nutmeg trees were cultivated by villagers and harvested for trade with outsiders. Thanks to the nutmeg, pepper, and other spices that grew wild in Indonesia, busy trade routes flourished in Indonesian seas long before the arrival of Europeans. Yet the items the Bandanese traded for, such as metal tools, would not feed them, and thus they had to pursue other activities, such as fishing, to feed their families.

A good way to study such diverse lifestyles is to organize them into categories—growing of rice and sago palm, the pulp of which natives ground into flour; gathering wild plants and fruits; fishing; hunting; growing crops for trade purposes; and the business of trading itself. Of the five categories, farming was probably the most important. Most indigenous farmers in the islands grew rice.

Farming on a Terrace

In well-populated areas, like central Java and Bali, rice was grown by way of a terrace system. Rice terraces, which looked like shelves, were cut in a stair-step fashion up the hillsides, and each terrace was kept flooded with water during the growing season. The Indonesian rice terrace system was a sight to behold, particularly for foreigners who had never traveled the islands before. Author Charles Corn, whose book *Scents of Eden* described the early days of the spice trade, describes the wonder that early Europeans often felt when viewing these terraces for the first time:

Within days they sighted the changing patterns of Java's great green and purple folds. From the decks the Mariners marveled at the terraced rice fields flashing in the sun against a nexus of austere, moss-colored mountains.[3]

Indonesian farmers cultivated rice using a terrace system like the one pictured here. This system ensured that each level remained flooded with water during the growing season.

Farmers in eastern and central Java, Bali, and other crowded islands had to use their fields again and again. The terraces, and the irrigation systems farmers set up to complement them, allowed tribesmen to plant crops in the same field again and again. Frank Clune, an Australian traveler and writer who visited Indonesia in the 1940s, noted just how economical the Javanese could be with the little bit of land available to them:

> Java is one of the most densely-populated islands in the world. . . . Little plots of land no bigger than a kitchen table, gouged out of the hillside and leveled off. . . . Other holdings, no bigger than a . . . backyard, support entire families.[4]

Rice farmers also knew how to take advantage of every food source that could be found on their rice terraces. Western observers have reported watching Balinese farmers trap and eat the freshwater eels that live in flooded rice fields. The Balinese set out woven basket traps for the eels at night and haul in their take in the morning.

Harvest Time

In sparsely populated areas like Kalimantan, farmers had room to move their crops to a new location whenever their fields became exhausted of nutrients. These tribes practiced a type of farming known as swidden agriculture, or slash-and-burn. Tribesmen would prepare the fields for planting by cutting and burning away brush and trees.

When it came time for the harvest, the Dayak peoples of Kalimantan in particular had an ancient and well-ordered ritual for processing their crop. Tribeswomen would pass the rice through a husking mill, a tool built in two parts and hollowed in the upper half. To husk the rice, the women would move the upper part of the mill to the left and to the right until the rice husk was ground away. The rice itself dropped through to a mat set beneath the mill.

Rice was an important crop, but so was the sago palm, which tribesmen either took wild from the forest or which they grew in their own plot. Sago was a primary food source for early tribes who did not grow rice and who also relied on hunting and gathering for sustenance.

A Tree of Life

The sago palm tree may have been the most useful plant in Indonesian history. Its strong, water-repellent leaves were used to roof homes and were folded into disposable spoons at mealtimes. Tribesmen cut off a thin part of the leaf to floss their teeth, and sago branches were woven into baskets. Yet the most important part of the sago was its wood, which tribesmen would turn into a flour used to make bread. Tribesmen processed the sago by felling the tree, cutting it in half, carving out its pulp, soaking the pulp until it turned into paste, and then making flour from the paste. A sago tree matured in twelve to fifteen years and once harvested provided a bounty for the family. Sago was still a food staple in the Molucca islands in the 1990s, when author Tim Severin watched a tribesman go through the painstaking process of making flour from sago pulp:

> The sago gatherer claimed that in just two days' work he could produce enough food to feed his family for a month. As for the sago palm, he said, once you had planted the seedling there was no more work involved. You merely had to let it grow.[5]

Sago palms were also a source of protein, thanks to the insect grubs that lived in the rotting trunks of fallen sago trees. These grubs were considered a delicacy and usually harvested for special feasts and festivals.

Sago was one of the few native plants that tribesmen planted, tended, and harvested themselves. Edible plants and fruits were so plentiful in the rain forests that a single day of gathering would produce enough food for several days.

Food from the Forest

Coconut palms, the nuts of which are edible, are probably the best known of Indonesia's many fruit trees. However, the gigantic durian tree bears fruit that is a particular favorite of indigenous tribesmen. The Mentawai had a gathering system by which they would send their most nimble members up the tree trunk. The remaining members of the group would stand at the bottom and catch whatever fruit the climbers might throw to them.

But gathering food in the forest involved much more than picking fruit and climbing trees. Anything edible was fair game to indigenous gatherers; the women of a tribe might build a fire next to a beehive, smoke out the bees, and remove honeycomb once the hive had emptied. Or they might capture small dragonflies and bring them home to be roasted over a fire until they were crunchy.

Caring for Livestock

Almost every indigenous tribe kept domestic animals, usually chickens, pigs, and buffalo, though the latter were more likely to be owned by rice farmers, who used them to pull wooden plows in their fields. Pigs about the size of miniature collies were undoubtedly the most important domestic animal in indigenous life; pork was a meal often reserved for special occasions, such as weddings or feasts, and thus domestic pigs were closely attended. The Korowai of Papua kept their pigs in their homes, which were built in trees high off the ground; the tribe rarely ate its own pigs, preferring to use them to settle disputes and to use as dowries when their daughters married.

The Mentawai let their pigs run wild in the forest near their villages but fed them regularly enough so that the pigs would not go off on their own. If the tribe moved to a new location, their pigs would go with them. Tribesmen caught the pigs in a

Indonesian women make flour from the pulp of a sago palm tree. The sago palm is considered the most useful plant in Indonesian history.

trap, strapped them in bags made from sago leaves, and hung them over their shoulders like backpacks. The Mentawai and other tribes also hunted wild pigs, which were common to Indonesia's rain forest.

Tribal Hunts

Historically, the jungles of Indonesia were also home to tigers, orangutans, rhinoceroses, elephants, and large monitor lizards. However, most indigenous hunters preferred smaller game. They hunted frogs,

A Dayak man uses a blowpipe to hunt monkeys in the canopy. Dayak hunters were skilled enough with the blowpipe to strike prey from great distances.

deer, pigs, monkeys, and even bats. Mentawai tribesmen turned their monkey hunts into journeys, leaving the women and children behind and setting up a separate campsite about a day's walk from the village. They hunted smaller species of monkey, such as macaques, with poisoned arrows. They would shoot at the monkeys in the trees, wait until one was hit, and then climb the tree to fetch the carcass. The monkey's skull was boiled in a soup and eaten by the hunters at their campsite. They smoked the remaining parts of the animal and brought these portions back to their families.

The Mentawai hunted with bows and arrows, but the Dayak hunted with blowpipes, hand-carved weapons that measured about six feet long and came equipped with a foot-long poisoned dart. The Dayak made the poison themselves from tree sap and snake venom. Dayak hunters were skilled enough with the blowpipe to hit an animal from a distance of fifty feet. The poison was rarely enough to kill the animal, but it disabled the prey long enough for the hunter to capture it and cut its throat.

Like other indigenous hunters, the Dayak hunted small game. They did, however, occasionally hunt crocodiles and large lizards. Killing a lizard usually required spearing it to death, but a crocodile hunt needed a trap and cunning. The Dayak made their trap by attaching a rattan rope to a stick sharpened at both ends. They would bend the stick in half, impale an animal carcass—usually of a pig or a monkey—on it, wrap the whole package in rattan, and hang it from a branch over the river.

Once the crocodile swallowed the bait, the waiting hunters pulled on the rattan so that the stick would snap open in the reptile's stomach, impaling it. The group then pulled the croc to the riverbank and let it die in the sun.

Food from the Waters

Women rarely engaged in tribal hunts, but most did fish, thus providing another important source of protein for their families. The Dayak often made fishing into a family affair. The village would choose a river or stream known to be rife with fish and then build a dam equipped with a small, central enclosure across a narrow section of the water. Once fish were trapped in the dam enclosure, Dayak warriors, women, children, and elderly would catch them with spears and nets.

Mentawai and Asmat women used nets to catch snails, freshwater mussels, and shrimp. Indigenous tribesmen who fished on the ocean were more likely to ply spears and fishing lines. The Bajau, a nomadic tribe that lived in the Philippines and Malaysia as well as Indonesia, depended almost entirely on fish for food. Fishing was a male activity among the Bajau, and tribesmen often fished by lantern light, using handheld lines to catch tuna, shark, and stingray.

The Whale Hunters

The Lamalera of the small island of Lembata are unique among indigenous fishermen in that they hunt whales, which are mammals, as well as fish. The Lamalera, who also grow some crops, including corn, focus on whale hunts each spring; they hunt several species of whale, including sperm whale. Usually only small male whales are taken; hunting a full-grown sperm whale, which can reach sixty feet, is considered too dangerous. Lamalera tribesmen also hunt shark, including the Great White and the Whale Shark, manta rays, marlin, and sun fish, but a whale is the most prized prey.

They fish with harpoons from thirty-foot boats, and the hunts are incredibly dangerous but also very exciting, as writer Fred Bruemmer found when he accompanied them on a whale hunt in 2001:

> At a sudden cry, the crew swings into action, rowing and paddling to the rapid cadence of time-honored chants. On his perch the harpooner is at ease, even when the boat pitches, slews and yaws in stormy weather. Finally he tenses and, in a great leap, flings himself on the prey and drives in the harpoon. . . . The harpooner always jumps onto the back of the whale, shark, or ray—such leaping greatly increases his accuracy and killing power.[6]

A Dangerous Undertaking

Once the fish or whale has been speared, the harpooner hauls himself back into the boat as quickly as possible, to avoid being attacked by the wounded and angry prey. The entire crew is put in danger at this point since a large shark or whale could easily smash their craft, and, indeed, the Lamalera have lost a good many boats and crew members during fishing and whaling expeditions.

As soon as the harpooner climbs back on board, the crew pulls the strong rope tied to the harpoon and hauls their catch to the surface. Since the harpoon rarely kills such large animals, crew members will then dive into the water, swim beneath the surface, and stab their catch to death with long-bladed, bamboo-handled knives.

If a whale or shark is taken, it is lashed alongside the boat and pulled to shore. Other fish, even large ones such as the manta ray, are brought aboard the boat and cut into chunks at sea. The final butchering is done on land with help from the rest of the tribe.

The tribe keeps about half the meat and fat for itself and uses the rest for barter. The women travel to a marketplace five miles away and trade with women from the mountain villages. Says Fred Bruemmer,

> Carrying heavy basins of meat and fat on their heads, they proceed straight-backed along a path used by untold generations. At the market, women from the mountain villages spread agricultural produce under the trees. [Lamaleran women] sit apart. . . . In the afternoon, [they] set off for home with basins of maize, rice, yams,

bananas, cassava and other fruits and vegetables.[7]

Farmers Who Fished

Traditionally, most indigenous farmers did not hunt, but many fished in inland rivers and on the ocean, although few experienced the danger that the Lamalera encountered in their hunts. A Jesuit priest enroute to China in 1698 described a village in Sumatra that successfully combined farming and fishing. The local peoples, who were Acehnese, lived in houses made of bamboo and palm leaves, raised cattle and fowl, and grew rice and fruit. The men of the village also spent a good deal of their time fishing, the priest reported:

Nothing is more delightful than to see in the morning, an endless stream of little fishing boats which leave the

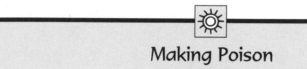

Making Poison

Indonesia's indigenous hunters have always made the poison that tipped their arrows and enabled them to hunt prey and fight enemies. The poison created by the Mentawai was always particularly feared and associated by those who knew the tribe with black magic. However, researcher Jean-Philippe Soulé observed the making of Mentawai poison while he lived with the tribe and discovered that the feared mixture was actually made of common jungle materials.

Tribesmen will harvest leaves from a rain-forest plant called a raggi, liquid from the wood of a Urat tree, and green chilies, which grow wild in the rain forest. The raggi leaves are pounded into a paste, which is then stored in a banana leaf that is closed up at the bottom by a strip of rattan. The Urat liquid and the chilies are added, and tribesmen complete the process with the help of rattan baskets and grinding. Much of the procedure is still kept secret, Soulé said.

The Mentawai tip their handmade arrows with poison and are careful not to knick or cut themselves while doing so. If the poison enters the bloodstream, it can kill them; however, if they eat a pig that has been killed by poison, they will not be harmed, because small amounts of the poison when ingested through the stomach are not lethal.

Mentawai poison *is* lethal enough to kill wild boars and deer almost instantly. But monkeys, a favorite prey of the Mentawai, are more resistant to it and may live up to five minutes; Mentawai hunters wait until the monkey collapses in a tree and then go to fetch the carcass.

Women from an Indonesian village sell spices at a local marketplace. Spices have been an important commodity in Indonesia for many centuries.

harbor at daybreak and only return in the evening at sunset. You would call it a swarm of bees returning to the hive laden with the fruits of their labor.[8]

The Acehnese were known as splendid sailors and determined traders; they controlled many of the sea routes that coursed beside their home in the northeastern corner of Sumatra. They were among many tribes that thrived and prof-

ited from Indonesia's centuries-old commercial trade.

Life on the Trade Winds

To understand Indonesian trade routes, one must first understand the regional climate. Thanks to the monsoon cycle, winds in Indonesia blow southwest and then northwest in a regular pattern, allowing ancient ships to sail from their home ports and then back again whenever the winds changed. More than a thousand years have passed since the first Chinese, Indian, and Arab traders ventured into Indonesian waters to trade for prized spices—nutmeg, mace, clove, and pepper—used to preserve food and make perfume and medicines.

Growing Spices

Nutmeg and clove trees and pepper bushes grew naturally in Indonesia's hot, tropical climate. Pepper was commonly grown in the Sumatran interior; clove trees grew on Ternate and Tidore, northern islands in the Molucca chain; and nutmeg grew on Banda Island in the southern end of the Moluccas, which were known as the Spice Islands. Spices were a particularly valuable commodity in the era before refrigeration, when they were used to season and preserve meat. Outsiders believed, wrongly, that these spices could only be grown in Indonesia and thus traveled many miles and paid a good deal in trade goods to obtain them.

Srivijaya

Wealthy and powerful kingdoms and states grew up around the spice trade and the shipping of Indonesian products, such as camphorwood, aloes, and pearls, to China, India, and Arabia. One of these kingdoms was Srivijaya of southeast Sumatra, which flourished from the seventh to the fourteenth century.

Srivijaya was a maritime power and handled international shipping in its harbor city, Palambang. Ships from elsewhere in the Indonesian archipelago traveled to Palambang to do their trading, and a traveler who arrived in Palambang in A.D. 671 reported seeing ships carrying Chinese porcelains, jade, and silks, and spices from the Molucca Islands.

Srivijayan culture bore the imprint of the many foreign traders that sailed in and out of its shores. Archaeologists have found Sanskrit writings, a language that came from India, and remnants of the monasteries that once made Srivijaya a center of Buddhist learning.

Srivijaya had been designated a Chinese vassal state in the sixth century A.D., meaning that it served as an intermediary between China and other less-favored states in the archipelago. Srivijaya fell out of favor with China and was stripped of its vassal status in 1380—but not before the kingdom had played its part in nurturing the Buddhist faith in the island region. Buddhism had taken root early in Srivijaya, and at one point more than one thousand Buddhist monks were studying in Palambang's monasteries.

Spice delivery routes grew up over land and sea. Pepper was grown inland by the Minangkabau and then taken by river raft to the coast. Spice traders on the Moluccas often traded with the Javanese for rice and sage, which did not grow on their islands, and with Asian and Arab traders for metal tools and medicine.

The Bandanese, as well as those who lived on Ternate and Tidore, learned early in their history to cultivate their own groves of spice trees so that their own families and villages would have enough product to trade.

Rhinoceros horns, believed to contain medicinal properties, were once lucrative products for Indonesian traders.

How a Tribe Got Its Name

The Minangkabau peoples of western Sumatra were at war with their longtime enemies, the Javanese, who lived in central and east Java. The two sides decided that in lieu of sending armies into battle, they would have a simple contest, involving buffalo, to determine which was the worthier tribe. The Javanese sent their largest champion buffalo to the battle, but the Minangkabau, determined to rely on cunning instead of force, chose a small calf. They tipped the calf's horns with steel and starved him for a day or two. On the day of the contest, both sides sent their buffalo out to fight. Since his opponent was only a calf, the large bull did not attack it. But the calf was by now very hungry and so ran toward the bull, hoping it might turn out to be a cow and provide him with some milk. As the calf ran under the bull, his steel-tipped horns struck the bull's belly and made a fatal wound.

There is no evidence that this contest ever took place. But the name Minangkabau means the "victorious buffalo," and the tribe regards the incident as the story of their origins. They also see it as an illustration of tribal attitude: Despite the fact that they were vastly outnumbered by their enemies, the Javanese, they were still wily enough to come out of the situation as winners.

They tended their nutmeg groves by clearing out undergrowth and removing dead or broken branches, and once the nutmeg fruit ripened, they processed nutmeg from the pit of the fruit and another spice, mace, from the dried fiber around the pit. Tribesmen then traded the nutmeg to those in the village who worked as traders, and those traders would in turn trade the nutmeg to outsiders.

Feathers from a Legendary Bird

Foreign traders acquired a host of other products from Indonesian forests and seas. Tree balsam, aloe, aromatic gums, and rhinoceros horn—which the Chinese believed to be an antidote for poison—were brought from the interior; pearls were harvested from Indonesian waters. Even the remote tribes in Papua, which occupies the western half of the island of New Guinea, engaged in trade, say historians.

Papuan tribesmen hunted birds of paradise, a species native to Indonesia, and wore its long beautiful plumes when they went into battle. Those who lived close enough to the Papuan coastline often encountered seagoing residents of the Aru and Kai Islands, which are located off the coastline of Papua. The Aru and Kai islanders traded for bird of paradise feathers and in turn traded them to Spice islanders. When European traders began frequenting the Spice Islands, they acquired these beautiful feathers and brought them to Europe, where they adorned knights' helmets.

Building Families and Culture

Indigenous hunters, farmers, gatherers, and fishermen worked hard and played hard, and they engaged in ancient cultural practices that varied like a kaleidoscope across the islands. Each tribal culture was individual and unique since tribes rarely had contact with outsiders, save for the traders they encountered on the coasts and inland waterways. However, as different as each tribe might be, they did have a number of cultural characteristics in common. Most of these tribes put the welfare of the group above that of the individual. And most tailored their culture and traditions to their surroundings.

Chapter 2

The Rhythms of Culture

Indonesian geography was so forbidding—miles of open oceans and impenetrable jungles—that many tribes, except for those who regularly engaged in trade, lived in total isolation. Thus the cultural practices and traditions that each tribe developed tended to be unique. For example, the Asmat, who lived in the forests of Papua, kept very different traditions than did the Javanese, who were rice farmers in central and east Java.

However, despite these geographic and cultural differences, tribal life and tradition were always geared towards the greater good, since tribesmen invariably depended on one another for survival. Communal ties were important in keeping the tribe healthy and safe, and so indigenous culture focused on strengthening those ties.

This need for a strong community was reflected in the way tribesmen built their homes, arranged their marriages, raised their children, and practiced their traditions. This does not mean, however, that

tribal life was dreary and filled with hardship. Tribes from Papua to Java also took time to create works of art, build homes that were distinctive as well as practical, and hold festive gatherings. Like Western and non-Western cultures around the world, Indonesia's tribesmen took care to experience joy whenever possible.

The House as Fortress

Many tribes, especially those who live in rain-forest areas, have a long history of conflict with their neighbors. These tribes regard their homes as a first line of defense against enemy attack as well as a place to live. The Batak of Sumatra feuded with each other for generations, and individual villages were surrounded by mounds of earth and brushwood that were in turn surrounded by an impenetrable hedge of prickly bamboo, camouflaging the homes inside.

The Korowai and Kombai raised their homes off the ground, sometimes as high as 150 feet, by building them in treetops. Historians believe that they were driven by enemies to live so high off the ground, though frequent flooding in their home territory must have played a part, too. Korowai and Kombai families even kept their dogs and pigs in their treetop homes.

Tribesmen took the extra caution of building mud-covered, lattice-strip platforms over holes in the floor of their tree houses, which served as fireplaces. If a fire should ever rage out of control, the platform could be dropped quickly through the hole and out of the home.

The Asmat, too, raised their homes above ground, as high as eight feet, though these homes rested on stilts, not tree branches. The Asmat also built tall watchtowers near their homes to keep a look out for enemies.

Living and Working Together

Asmat homes were bamboo longhouses that boasted thatched roofs and bark-covered floors and were big enough to house an entire forest band. Catholic missionaries who have ministered to the tribe since the 1950s report that a traditional Asmat home may contain as many as sixteen fireplaces, one for each family in the longhouse. Thus a group of Asmat may live and work together, but cooking is still an individual event, with each family gathering around its fireplace to eat.

These missionaries also theorized that a tradition of communal housing developed because constructing a house by hand in a jungle setting was too strenuous an activity for an individual or family to tackle alone. In indigenous society every able-bodied person must hunt for food, gather plants

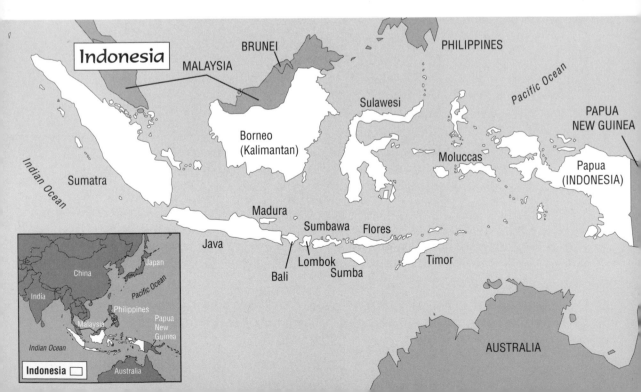

An Indonesian family poses outside their raised home. Many indigenous people still build raised homes for protection against frequent flooding.

An Indonesian fisherman displays his catch. In traditional indigenous society, men and women share the responsibility of providing food for the family.

and fruit, tend crops, or care for children each day. In such a setting, individuals cannot devote much time to building a house. Therefore, communal homes became the norm. Those who have studied the Asmat also point out that, for this tribe, communal homes have another practical use: If many families live together, elderly members can look after young children while the adults are out hunting or gathering food.

The Dayak also lived in longhouses, but theirs had individual rooms, one per family. Three to fifty Dayak families might live in a single longhouse, and a medium-sized Dayak village might contain three longhouses. But daily life and activity centered not in the house itself but on the veranda-like structure the Dayak built along the house's exterior. Although Western-style homes have become more common throughout Indonesia and in Dayak territory, some Dayak families still prefer to live in traditional longhouses. Travel writer and adventurer Tracy Johnston, while on a river-rafting trip in Kalimantan during the 1990s, visited and described some of these dwellings:

The dark ironwood longhouses we were ushered into were like all the Dayak longhouses I'd read about: huge and raised perhaps six feet off the ground. . . . The covered veranda, which ran the length of the house, could have been a boardwalk on Main Street. It was made of weathered wood planks and the villagers clearly used it to meet and chat. Women were husking rice on it in huge wooden mortars and sifting the grain in round, flat baskets.[9]

Souvenirs and Sculpture

Dayak homes were also known for the grisly ornaments that hung over each family's fireplace, as writer Edwin H. Gomes discovered while visiting the Dayak early in the twentieth century.

Over [the family's fireplace] hangs the most valuable ornament in the eyes of the Dayak, the bunch of human heads. These are the heads obtained when on the warpath by various members of the family . . . and are handed down from father to son.[10]

Other indigenous tribal homes were decorated with much less grisly mementos. The Toraja, a rice farming tribe in Sulawesi, carved animals, such as buffalo heads, and birds, leaves, and other important tribal symbols onto the wood exterior of their homes. A Toraja home always faced north, the direction that the tribe associated with its ancestors. Toraja homes were surrounded by rice-storage barns as well as a small platform that

served as a common meeting place. There Torajan women might weave cloth while the men repaired tools. Any guests the household might have for the evening would sleep on this platform.

The Balinese, as well as their guests, spent most of their time outdoors. The Balinese lived with their spouses, children, and extended family in a walled compound filled with a series of wooden structures. These structures included open pavilions, a family temple, bedroom areas, a kitchen, and a granary.

Balinese husbands and wives usually slept in the same room, but many tribes demanded that women and men, whether married or single, sleep separately. Well-to-do Javanese households usually put the women and children in the same rooms, and the husbands slept elsewhere in the house. The entire family used a common area in the house for ceremonies.

Such strict rules for interaction between the sexes also governed tribal courtship and marriage. In most indigenous societies, the Western ideas of love and romance did not apply. Marriages represented not so much private declarations of romantic love as a way to cement loyalties between groups and strengthen bonds between families.

Arranging a Marriage

Marriage was considered so important by some indigenous tribesmen that their men and women would marry as early as possible. A Balinese youth, for example, could not expect to assume important village positions until he had taken a wife and fathered children. Thus, finding a mate was serious business in Bali and elsewhere and rarely left up to the individuals involved; more often than not, the couple's families would arrange a marriage.

Negotiations for a marital union could be quite complicated. The Kedang, who live on Lembata, had a lengthy gift-giving ritual that lasted years and was known to continue even if one or both spouses died before completion of the process. The children of such a marriage finished the ritual themselves, since the marriage would not be "finalized" until the gift-giving had been completed.

The bride's and groom's families gave gifts back and forth according to a formalized pattern. The bride's family usually received offerings like bronze gongs and elephant tusks, whereas the groom's family received cloth that the bride had dyed and woven herself.

Marriages were arranged for many reasons. The families involved might wish to increase their personal wealth and power, or they might be looking to keep the peace when a dispute arose. When two Mentawai villages feuded, for example, two of their residents would marry so that tempers would be soothed, an alliance built, and rivalry between the two sides subside.

Polygamy was practiced in many parts of Indonesia but never required, except among wealthy and powerful families. When a Javan or Sumatran king married,

he did so to acquire allies and power, writes Jean Gelman Taylor, author of *Indonesia, Peoples and Histories:*

> [The king] took into his household women who were daughters of all classes of men: princes, nobles, army commanders, vanquished princes, village heads, religious teachers, artisans. The daughters born from the king's liaisons could be distributed to other men. . . . Men receiving a wife from the king could boast of enjoying royal favor.[11]

An Element of Choice

More often than not, a bride and groom were not given a choice as to whom they might marry. Some cultures, however, did allow their young people some freedom. Western visitors to Bali reported that it was not unusual to find an attractive Balinese girl surrounded by boys who wished to court her and bring her small gifts. A male of the Tanahmerah tribe in Papua could marry the woman of his choice, but first he had to buy her with shells, animal's teeth, or other items of value. Single Tanahmerah men and women were not supposed to "date" one another before marriage, but missionaries to the tribe reported that surreptitious courtships did occur.

Among the Asmat a girl was expected to marry the man her parents chose for her. If she refused, they would berate her until she gave in. However, missionaries

A young couple is wed in a traditional Balinese marriage ceremony. Marriages in traditional Indonesian society were typically arranged.

to the Asmat have reported that determined couples were known to elope. But even an arranged marriage did not have to be an unhappy one, as Malcolm S. Kirk wrote when he traveled through the Papuan jungle:

> It is not unusual to see a fierce-looking warrior tenderly holding the hand of a wife who married him because the parents had arranged the union.[12]

Finery and Feasting

Like Westerners, indigenous Indonesian tribes have a host of rituals reserved strictly for marriage ceremonies. Tribal ceremonies could be quite elaborate and beautiful. A traditional Balinese bride was a sight to behold: Covered head to toe in finery, she wore golden ornaments and a headdress, and clothing lined with silver brocade. An Asmat bride dressed much more simply, in feathers and furs, and the Asmat wedding

The Art of Cloth Making

Batik cloth, most commonly made by Javanese artisans, is traditionally created by hand with a technique that involves wax and natural dyes. Traditional batik involved white, handwoven cloth with patterns of deep blue derived from the indigo plant. Later patterns also incorporated other colors like dark brown, a dye derived from palm tree bark.

To make batik, the artisan drew outlines of a design on a piece of cloth woven on a loom. The pattern drawn would likely include flower petals, loops, and curls. Once he decided what kind of design he wanted, the artisan stretched the cloth on a bamboo frame and outlined his work with wax. The artisan then dipped the cloth in dye, knowing that the dye would not affect the waxed parts of the cloth. When the cloth had dried, some wax would be scraped away and the batik dipped again, usually in a different color.

Depending on what kind of effect he was looking for, the artisan might add more wax, dip the cloth again, dye it, and scrape wax away until a complicated pattern of many colors emerged. Artisans were lent a helping hand during the eighteenth century by the invention of the *tjanting*.

The *tjanting* is a lamp-shaped tool with a bowl in which the wax could be kept in a liquid state. The *tjanting* had a fine spout through which the wax could be easily poured in ever more intricate patterns on the cloth. This new tool gave artisans more flexibility when they created their designs, and many were able to infuse an individual style to their batik through the *tjanting's* help.

was conducted much like a game with set rules.

The bride's mother wailed loudly at the prospect of losing her daughter to marriage, despite the fact that she herself had taken a leading role in arranging that marriage. All those who attended the wedding took care to wear a long face, particularly the bride and groom; tradition dictated that the couple not smile during the ceremony. Also, the groom was expected to make a mock "dash" for freedom. But his friends, in on the joke, would "capture" him and return him to his bride.

When a Yali marriage was celebrated, the centerpiece of the feast was always a pig roast. The Yali wore their best finery when celebrating a tribal marriage—shell necklaces and jewelry made from pig's teeth, and women wore bird of paradise feathers in their hair.

Work and Play for the Old and Young

Children in an Indonesian community live a life filled with pleasure and responsibility. They play games, roll in the mud, and splash in the ocean or a nearby stream or river. Yet children, just like the adults of the tribe, have jobs to do. Even today, when many children must attend school, families who still practice traditional ways see to it that their children pitch in whenever possible.

From an early age tribal children are assigned whatever task they are deemed physically able to do. Children of rice farm-

ers accompany their mothers in the field; in the forest, they follow along while their mothers pick plants and fruit. Both boys and girls spend most of their time with their mothers and female relatives while they are very young, and it is the women who teach them the work they must accomplish once they are older. The exceptions to this rule are hunting and warfare, which are taught by men.

Both boys and girls assume a good deal of responsibility at an early age. Mentawai girls, for example, are considered old enough at age ten to gather food in the jungle by themselves, sometimes staying away for days at a time. Mentawai boys are taught by the men of the tribe to hunt as soon as they are old enough to hold a bow and arrow.

A tribe's most respected teachers are also among its oldest. Elderly men and women of the tribe pass on important skills to the younger generation. Like the children, tribal elders carry a lighter work load than the village's more able-bodied adults. Still, even they are expected to work when they are able and contribute to the community. The older women might help care for children or mend fishing nets. Among the Lamalera, older men are expected to abandon their leisure activities and join their younger compatriots on the beach whenever a successful whaling crew returns home:

[For the] Lamalera, life is lived on the seashore. . . . Old men sit in the shade, smoking thin cigarettes rolled with strips of lontar palm leaf, talking about long-ago hunts, weaving new sails, or braiding new ropes. But the instant a boat rides in on a soaring swell, all the males, from tots to aged men, rush to help haul the boat up onto the beach.[13]

The elderly also assumed the important task of imparting tribal history, legends, and folklore.

Tribal Music and a Forest Dance

Indigenous music of the Indonesian islands revolves around rhythm. In Bali, musicians still play drums, gongs, xylophones, and metallophones, which look like xylophones but are made of metal instead of wood.

The Asmat, too, made music from drums, and historically Asmat drum making was a difficult and lengthy process. An Asmat drum maker hollowed out a log and carved it into an hourglass shape, cutting decorative symbols on the outer wood as he did so. He would then stretch lizard skin across the top of the drum, secure it by a string of rattan hoop, and then place it by a fire to dry.

Many complicated and beautiful dances evolved to accompany Indonesia's rhythmic music. In Bali, women performed the *legong,* which is like a ballet. Balinese dance also told sto-

An elderly Indonesian man carries a shark he has caught. Tribal elders are expected to contribute to the community if they are able.

ries about tribal gods, demons, and witches. The *ketjiak,* or monkey dance, performed by male dancers, was a particular favorite. A chorus of men would portray the army of monkeys that figured in a popular Balinese folktale. In this story, the monkey "army" rescued the wife of a Balinese god from a demon.

The Iban, a subtribe of the Dayak, performed a dance in honor of its sacred bird, the hornbill. The hornbill is a long-tailed, large-beaked bird almost as large as a swan. Johnston, during her river trip in Kalimantan, observed a hornbill dance during her sojourn with the Dayak:

A woman appeared onstage with a clutch of the hornbill's eighteen-inch-long tail feathers spread out between her fingers, and like the stately leisurely flight of the bird, she twisted

Shadow Puppets

The art of shadow puppet theater, or *wayang kulit,* came to the Indonesian islands by way of India. Commonly performed by the Javanese and Balinese peoples, shadow puppetry involved a puppeteer sitting behind an illuminated screen. He would hold elaborately designed, flat puppets mounted on long rods so that they cast shadows on the screen. He would then manipulate the puppets to tell his story, and the audience could see only their shadows.

Shadow puppets were traditionally made out of buffalo hide and painted with gold and other bright colors. The puppets had elongated necks and arms, the latter of which were jointed so they could be manipulated by the puppeteers. Shadow puppet plays told stories and legends familiar to the indigenous peoples, so most of the characters were easily recognizable. Good puppets were designed with almond eyes and pointed noses, whereas villainous puppets had bulging eyes and bulbous noses.

The puppeteer, known as a *dalang,* narrated his story in a singsong voice. Puppet shows were often lengthy and could last all night if the audience was willing. In ancient times shadow puppets were believed to be the souls of the dead. The puppeteer served as an intermediary between them and the living as he told his story. Shadow puppet theater was considered holy, and even in modern times the burning of incense and prayers mark performances.

Shadow puppetry took on a more radical form during World War II while Indonesia was occupied by the Japanese. Instead of relying on traditional stories, *dalangs* would use the puppets to critique the government, and Japanese officials unfamiliar with shadow puppet theater remained none the wiser.

Many Indonesian tribes regularly held festivals to celebrate the importance of the sago palm tree.

and dipped in measured movements, using her entire body to simulate the bird's grace.[14]

Frolic and a Unique Ritual

Festivals and gatherings could be held for any number of reasons: a religious occasion, family reasons, or celebration of a favorite food. Sago festivals were held by Korowai, Kombai, and other tribes who depend on the sago as a diet staple. However, the focus of festivities is not the sago itself but the grubs, or insect larvae, that grow inside them. Women of the tribe would harvest the grubs from rotted sago palm logs and roast them for a feast. Both men and women would want to look their best for the festival, which included chanting and dancing in addition to eating. Korowai women shaved their heads bald with a bamboo razor and pierced their noses with batwing bones. Korowai men were fond of tattoos, which they would apply with heated wooden tongs.

European explorers knew the Dayak as a people that loved a good time. Europeans who penetrated Kalimantan's forests early in Indonesian history returned home with stories of rice wine, dancing, and silliness at Dayak gatherings that lasted all night. Contemporary Western visitors have since learned that these early explorers did not exaggerate. In 1976 American adventurer Eric Hansen visited the Dayak and partook in a party game that Westerners would find bizarre to say the least. Johnston describes Hansen's encounter in *Shooting the Boh:*

[Hansen] was given a live rooster and told to hit every man, woman and child in the longhouse over the head with it. He started out giving people little taps but one woman took the rooster from him and demonstrated how to do it right: grab the bird by the legs and swing it like a tennis racket. She demonstrated sizzling backhands and overhead smashes. By the time Hansen was finished everyone was roaring with laughter and the rooster was dead.[15]

As the night wore on, Johnston wrote, Hansen watched the gathering grow ever more riotous and memorable: "Guns were fired into the jungle; men, women and children got sick over the longhouse railings . . . and finally the entire longhouse caught fire."[16]

Although this treatment of an animal is inhumane by Western standards, the purpose of the activity, accompanied as it was by laughter, does not seem to exhibit cruelty. Indeed, domestic animals like chickens and pigs are too valuable a source of protein to be used lightly. Although Hansen never learned exactly what the ritual

A Tribe Run by Women

The indigenous tribes of Indonesia were for the most part patrilineal, meaning that an individual received properties, titles, or authority through his father's family. A notable exception to this rule was the Minangkabau of Sumatra.

The Minangkabau traced their lineage through the women in the family and placed all houses and lands under female control. Minangkabau women farmed on family-owned land and did not depend on their husbands for food and shelter. In fact, they did not even live with their husbands; a Minangkabau man had "visiting" rights to his wife and children in her home, which she shared with her kin. He would live elsewhere, perhaps in a home belonging to his sisters; it was not uncommon for the sisters in a family to assume ownership of the home and lands and then to work the fields along with their brothers.

Tribal wives fed and cared for their children without their husbands' help, although they, like the Minangkabau men, benefited from trade with the outside world. The women would grow pepper for export and also prepare goods that their men brought in from the forest so that the wood, aloes, or other products could then be sold in trade.

Not surprisingly, Minangkabau men became known as wanderers who left their territory to seek opportunities elsewhere. Some Minangkabau men even studied at Islamic schools in Aceh and Banten. Most Minangkabau tribesmen eventually converted to Islam, just as most of Indonesia did. However, despite the fact that Islam is a male-dominated religion, the Minangkabau still continued their tradition of matrilineal families.

meant, flogging tribe members with a rooster surely had its place in Dayak culture.

Keeping Order, Making War

Despite the occasional frivolity, indigenous tribesmen kept an undercurrent of seriousness in their daily lives. All tribesmen knew that there was a specific way to do things and a specific way to behave. These rules and regulations were ultimately enforced by tribal government, and that same government also, at times, had to be defended from external enemies. And war, like everything else, had rules that had to be followed.

Chapter 3

Going to War, Keeping the Peace

As with most things in Indonesia, the environment in which each tribe lived influenced how the people governed themselves. A village of rice farmers lived a more settled existence than did a tribe that relied mostly on hunting; thus farmers often preferred a much more structured government. Hunters, on the other hand, lived a democratic existence more suited to a somewhat nomadic lifestyle. A farming village located in a region governed by a powerful ruler, such as a kingdom in Sumatra and Java, also contended with an extra layer of bureaucracy. Chiefs in these villages acted as intermediaries between the people and their rulers, levying taxes and carrying out the king's orders.

Keeping the tribe safe from enemies was a duty that consumed every adult male. Other than hunting, growing food, or fathering children, going to war was the most important thing a man could do for his people. In most tribes a mystique even grew around the warrior. A boy did not become a man, many felt, until he had killed an enemy in battle.

A warrior knew that he upheld an important and ancient tradition. The tools and rituals of war—weapon making, cannibalism, head-hunting—were as much a part of indigenous culture as cloth making, dances, or wedding ceremonies.

Chiefs in Charge

Village chiefs, or headmen, in Sumatra, Java, Bali, and elsewhere served as representatives of the royal court if the area was governed by a king or sultan. One of their primary duties for the court was to collect taxes, which were then turned over to the ruler. Later in Indonesia's history, when colonial government supplanted the native kings, headmen took on other responsibilities; they oversaw crews that built roads and bridges. And when the Dutch implemented a monetary system, the chiefs saw to it that villagers purchased a certain amount of local product each year: pepper, rattan, and cotton, a crop that the Dutch introduced to the islands.

But villagers had little contact with their king or with their Dutch rulers and probably felt little connection to them, even when they were being threatened by an enemy, as Zainu'ddin writes:

> During wars, the villages suffered through disrupted communications and the destruction of crops. Apart from that the villagers probably had a greater sense of identity with their village community than with (the king).[17]

Village headmen also settled disputes; on the island of Banda, such headmen were known as the Orang Kaya, or rich men. Each island had its own Orang Kaya; unlike nearby Ternate and Tidore, the Banda were not a kingdom. The islands were organized much more democratically, with each Orang Kaya governing his own community and occasionally warring with his neighbors. But Banda's headmen were more likely to be involved with local issues than outside conflict. Their primary duties were organizing religious ceremonies and allocating rights to the valuable Bandanese nutmeg trees.

Solving Forest Disputes

Tribes in Kalimantan, Papua, and Sumatra relied primarily on hunting and tended to be seminomadic in their habits. Such tribes were much more democratic in their decision making, experts say. Anthropologists who have studied the Mentawai, for exam-ple, report that they had no organized political leadership. Rather, tribal matters and problems were handled via discussions between neighbors.

Practicality usually ruled the day: For example, hoarding food or some other item the tribe might need was all but unforgivable to the Mentawai. Indeed, the Mentawai shared meals with one another, and eating alone was strongly discouraged. Thus a member of the tribe who would not share was considered a difficult person and unwelcome in the community. But instead of punishing a hoarder, the Mentawai preferred a more pragmatic approach. If a tribesman would not share with the village he or she currently lived in, perhaps he or she would share with another. Thus the hoarder could be asked—or in some cases, convinced—to move out of the village, take along family members or anyone else who wished to go with him, and establish a new village somewhere else.

Other forest tribes took creative approaches to settling disputes. The Dayak devised a competition called a Besalam. They used the Besalam when individuals or families had a disagreement and could find no other means to settle it. When the Besalam method was chosen, each party "hired" a diver, a Dayak so good at holding his breath underwater that he could do so at competition levels. The Dayak learned to swim at an early age traditionally and some trained themselves to spend considerable amounts of time underwater. The most talented of these divers found themselves in demand as Besalam competitors, and most had handlers, who coached them during competition.

The feuding parties, their respective divers, and the divers' handlers would meet down at the local river. Each diver took a deep breath and dipped his head below the water's surface; as the divers held their breaths, often for several minutes, the antagonists would pass the time by waving fighting roosters at each other and throwing rice around. Westerners who have observed the Besalam ritual report that it usually continued until the divers were near death. Both divers kept their heads submerged until they lost consciousness. The diver who "won" was the last to be hauled out by his handler, unconscious but still alive; it was thus ultimately up to the handlers to estimate the stamina of their charges. In any case, whichever party had been aligned

A Mentawai tribesman paddles his dugout canoe. Unwelcome members of the Mentawai community were sometimes forced to leave the village.

with the last Dayak to be pulled alive from the water won the dispute.

Creating a Family for the Sake of Peace

When the Asmat fought, their opponents were usually neighboring villages. If hostile villages wanted to end conflict and ally with one another for friendship and protection, they would arrange what can only be described as an adult adoption. Members of the one tribe would adopt specific members of the other, and then all would be "family."

Indonesian villagers sell dried tobacco leaves at a market. Tobacco was sometimes used to settle tribal disputes.

Adults who had agreed to be adopted would arrive at the village where the adoption was to take place and spend the next several days behaving like children. Their adopted "mothers" rocked them to sleep in their arms, and the adoptees would pretend to nurse at their "mothers'" breasts. The adopted women pretended to learn how to fish again; the men "relearned" the art of hunting. Both sexes played games with the village youngsters.

The most important ritual of all was the rebirthing process. Sago leaves would be woven into the adoptees' hair, cane strips tied around their waists, and ochre and lime paint applied to their faces. The village women would stand in a line, their legs spread apart, and the men stood beside them. The adoptees would crawl through the corridor of women's legs to symbolize that they were being born again. When all the rituals were finished, the adoptees returned to their home village. But the newly established familial ties between the villages would continue.

A Tribal Justice

When disputes went beyond the disagreement stage and Besalam or adoption were no longer an option, punishments had to be administered. The Balinese even held a formal court with village headmen acting as judges and levying punishment for serious crimes like thievery. Other tribes dispensed justice in a more informal fashion. Charles Lindsay, author of *Mentawai Shaman, Keeper of the Rain Forest*, describes how Mentawai justice often demanded compensation for the victim and negotiation between the two parties. In his book, Lindsay tells the story of a Mentawai tribesman who lost his pet bat to hungry young neighbors. In the story the plaintiff was named Tumbu and he had kept a fruit bat, a so-called flying fox, as a pet for seven years:

> It seems, [that] three girls were passing by Tumbu's hut while nobody was home. The girls stole, cooked and ate the pet bat. . . . Tumbu tapped into local gossip, [and] learned who the rascals were; he later negotiated a damage settlement of tobacco.[18]

Justice among the Mentawai can also be self-administered. Lindsay tells of a Mentawai hunter who carelessly left behind one of his poisoned arrows when he left the village to go on a hunt. The man's son played with the arrow and died from the poison. When the man returned home and discovered what had happened, he felt obligated to take his own life.

Mentawai do not require suicide in such matters. But if the man Lindsay wrote of had not committed suicide, he more than likely would have been held responsible for his actions in some other way. If the stricken boy had not been his own son, the man's possessions might have been seized in retribution by the victim's family.

Murder is by far the worst crime an indigenous tribesman can commit. The Yali of Papua administer the ultimate punishment by executing the perpetrator and eating his flesh.

When a Tribe Goes to War

Indigenous tribes most commonly went to war to defend their villages or hunting grounds or territory they felt belonged to them, to settle old grudges or disputes that might simmer for generations between tribes, or to exact revenge for a wrong.

British soldiers found out just how exacting Javanese revenge could be when they took over a fort on Java that the Dutch, their colonial predecessors, had abandoned. Unbeknownst to them, during their tenure in that fort the Dutch had enraged the local tribesmen by assaulting their women. When white soldiers one day reappeared at the fort, tribesmen assumed that the Dutch had returned. They staged a nighttime raid against the fort, shooting flaming arrows to burn out the soldiers. The British survived the attack and in the morning staged a march with the British flag and colors so that the locals would know that this army came from a different European country.

The raid against the fort was a typical indigenous attack: Tribesmen engaged in short skirmishes rather than full-fledged battles. But the armies commanded by Indonesia's kings were an exception to this rule. The Dutch, as they battled for supremacy in the islands, fought a full-pitched battle with the ruler of Bali, known as the Radja, and his nobles in 1906. Zainu'ddin describes the battle in her book *A Short History of Indonesia:*

The fighting was fierce, the Balinese ruler and his nobles preferring annihilation to surrender. When the capital . . . fell, the local Radja, with his family and followers, dressed in their courtly regalia and each armed with a [sword] advanced to certain death. When the Radja was shot dead, his wives stabbed themselves.[19]

Tools of War

The royal armies of Indonesia commanded elephants specially trained for battle, cannons built by metalworkers who toiled in the kingdom, and a daggerlike weapon, the kris. In indigenous society the kris was a work of art as well as a weapon. The artisans who made them forged intricate patterns on their blades and handles.

But most indigenous tribes did not live under a king or field large armies. However, almost all of them fought with handmade weapons, some of which are also considered works of art. Dayak warriors in Kalimantan fought with spears, blowpipes, and machete-like swords called *mandaus*. The Tanahmerah of Papua went to war with spears and bamboo arrows tipped with hardwood, a feature that made them more lethal. The Nias, who lived in Sumatra, created swords shaped like a set of crocodile teeth. The Asmat armed themselves with bamboo knives and large, spectacular shields. Asmat warriors took a great deal of time carving their shields. They stained them with colors made from ochre and lime and cut designs

The Elephant in War

The Asian elephant and its African cousin were instruments of war as early as 300 B.C. Some historians refer to the war elephant as the military's first tank since it served the same purpose: It carried soldiers into battle and protected them at the same time.

Asian elephants are native to Indonesia but from earliest times were usually possessions of the wealthy; poorer families did not have the resources to feed such a large animal. They were often owned by kings and used for both ceremonies and war. European leaders who clashed with Indonesian indigenous kings and sultans wrote occasionally of the great war elephants manned by the royal armies.

War elephants were a scare tactic as well as military transportation. Armies

who had never fought against troops mounted on elephants were likely to panic and run at the sight of them. Some armies even tipped their elephants' tusks with spikes and shielded their already tough skin with heavy leather wraps. But once soldiers became accustomed to dealing with elephants, they learned quickly how to turn an elephant charge into a stampede. According to ancient accounts, elephants panicked very easily at unexpected occurrences. If soldiers brandished fire at them or sent a rain of arrows their way, the elephants were likely to turn and stampede through the ranks of their own army, thus defeating the purpose of having elephant troops in the first place.

in them that symbolized some familiar aspect of the world, such as pig tusks.

A Memory of Loved Ones, a Call for Revenge

The Asmat specialized in another tool of war that never saw the battlefield. These artists, also the tribe's warriors, sculpted what was known as an ancestor pole from tall tree trunks. These poles require weeks of work and are carved in a bark-floored ceremonial house known as a *jeu*.

Ancestor poles depict the maker's blood relatives who died violent deaths that must

be avenged; thus, the poles were a grisly reminder of a warrior's duty. Each time he saw the pole, anthropologists say, a warrior remembered the relatives whose deaths he would someday have to avenge.

Head-Hunting and Cannibalism

But the Asmat were headhunters as well as artists, and head-hunting frequently played a part in their vengeful raids. Asmat warriors would remove an enemy's head after they killed him and then eat his flesh. A tribal member gave this account of a head-hunting

47

A headhunter from Papua New Guinea poses with human skulls on pikes. Indonesian head-hunting tribes believed that the severed head of an enemy carried special powers.

episode to *National Geographic* writer Malcolm S. Kirk when he visited the Asmat in the 1960s:

The raiders cut off the victims' heads and limbs with bamboo knives and brought the dismembered bodies back to [the village]. The women accompanied their husbands and the bodies to the ceremonial house, where witnesses related how each head was taken. Then the heads were baked and the skin removed. The brains, shaken out through a hole cut in the temple, were eaten. The lower jaw was severed and worn on a necklace.[20]

The Asmat believed that the best way to tap an enemy warrior's strength and power was to eat his brains. But they were hardly the only tribe in Indonesia to headhunt and engage in cannibalism. Anthropologists who have studied the islands conclude that these practices were widespread, particularly in the rain forest.

When a Dayak brought an enemy head home to hang above his fireplace, he would impale it on a stick and smoke it over a fire before it became an ornament. The Yali of Papua ate the flesh of warriors they killed in battle, and the Batak even had a favorite "recipe" for cooking human flesh: lightly broiled and seasoned with salt and hot chili paste.

When Tanahmerah tribesmen took the head of an enemy, it would be skinned and dried and its scalp worn as an ornament by the warrior who had taken it.

The Siege of Ternate

Hairun, sultan of Ternate, had had a friendly relationship with Portuguese officials who kept a fort on Ternate and engaged in the spice trade for many years. But in 1570 the Portuguese army had a new captain to command their Ternate fort. Captain Mesquita, a brutal man who hated Muslims, lured the Muslim Hairun into the fort and separated him from his followers. Soldiers under Mesquita's command stabbed the sultan to death and displayed his head on a pike for all to see. Portuguese officials were furious with Mesquita's actions and sent him home in chains. However, this action was not enough to save the remaining Portuguese soldiers. The Ternate army, led by Hairun's son, Baab, and aided by neighboring is-

landers, laid siege to the fort for five years, preventing anyone from coming or going. When the Portuguese finally surrendered, most of their men were dead of starvation or disease. The survivors had lived on whatever rats, cats, or fruit bats they could catch.

Baab let the survivors go, but only on the condition that Portugal abandon its fort. On July 15, 1575, the Portuguese surrendered the island that they had kept a presence on for sixty-three years. But seven years later the Portuguese got their revenge. In 1582 Baab was lured onto a Portuguese ship where he was beheaded, drawn, and quartered. But his son, Said, managed to get the warrior's remains back to be buried on Ternate.

Sir Thomas Raffles

During the brief period of time that Great Britain oversaw Dutch interests in Indonesia, Thomas Stamford Raffles was sent to the Dutch settlement of Batavia, in Java, as the new colonial overseer. A controversial figure both then and now, Raffles attempted to institute a series of reforms, with mixed results. Raffles tried to abolish slavery, close gambling houses and cockfighting rings, institute a smallpox vaccination program, and clean up Batavia's canals, which were littered with refuse, much of it human. Raffles blamed much of Indonesia's violence on gambling and cockfighting: Four or five Indonesians or Chinese might be murdered in a single day over gambling debts. Raffles also took preemptive action against hostile Javanese kings, deposing one of them, Hamenkubuwono II, and installed a friendlier monarch in his place. These latter actions left much bitterness in their wake.

But Raffles, only thirty years old when he arrived in Java, had somewhat of an affinity for the Javanese people. He realized they were not inherently lazy, as the Dutch had believed. No people that had built rice terraces and engineered the flooding of the fields could be considered lazy, he said. He decreed that the Javanese should henceforth be paid rent for their agricultural land. Raffles also learned all he could about Javanese history, antiquities, and culture.

Raffles strongly opposed returning Indonesia to the Dutch. But Great Britain ignored his advice and in the post–Napoleonic era treaty-signing gave Indonesia back to Holland and called Raffles back from Batavia.

As colonial overseer of Batavia, Sir Thomas Stamford Raffles attempted to institute a series of sweeping reforms.

The rest of the victim's body would be roasted over a fire and eaten by the villagers.

Europeans who traveled to Indonesia and witnessed head-hunting and cannibalism had mixed reactions to these practices. The Jesuit priest Francis Xavier, who served as a Catholic missionary in the Indonesian islands for a number of years, was revolted by both the people and their traditions, as he would note in a letter to a colleague:

> The people [of Indonesia] are a very barbarous lot and full of treachery . . . and extremely disagreeable. . . . These are islands whose folk eat the bodies of enemies killed in tribal wars.[21]

Sir Thomas Raffles, an Englishman who governed Indonesia for a brief period in the nineteenth century, took a different view of these rituals, comparing them to the punishments and tortures that the English inflicted on their prisoners at one point in their history:

> However horrible eating a man may sound in European ears, I question whether the [person] suffers so much, or the punishment itself is worse than the European tortures of [long ago].[22]

A Warrior Culture Continues

Head-hunting and cannibalism have been outlawed in Indonesia for years, yet a warrior "attitude" persists among certain tribes, probably because going to war was one of the ways a boy became a man. Tribes that took heads and ate human flesh considered those practices a rite of passage for their young men: in other words, a youth did not become a man until he had killed a warrior in battle and brought home the head. Until a few decades ago a Tanahmerah man was not allowed to marry until he had taken at least two heads. When he and his bride came together to be married, he would place the two heads upon her outstretched arms; this gruesome practice was a required part of the ceremony.

Such old traditions have ensured that the need to fight and prove oneself in battle has endured in many island cultures, even as younger tribesmen became more Westernized. Explains an American who lived in Indonesia for thirty years,

> Clan loyalty is important. If you don't fight, you can be branded a coward, a traitor. The young people grow up hearing their elders talk about the great wars. Then they want to go out and fight, too.[23]

Even though head-hunting and cannibalism are now illegal in Indonesia, indigenous tribesmen still evoke rituals and dances associated with these ancient war rituals. While in Kalimantan, Johnston witnessed a Dayak dance performed by a man dressed in tree bark, animal skins, feathers, and shells. He carried a painted wooden shield and *mandau* and evoked the stance of an ancient warrior as he danced:

With [the Dayak's] first movement it was clear we were about to see some extraordinary dancing. Slowly, he twisted into an attack position—knees bent, fingers and toes spread out, neck in conscious counter-point—and then he whirled as if in flight, or battle, keeping his intense muscular control but capturing a feeling of frenzy or abandon. . . . The dance was a perfect translation of violence into grace.[24]

Rituals and Spirits

The rituals of head-hunting and cannibalism were governed by an unseen world—the world of the spirits. Tribesmen believe that all lives and all things are overseen by spirits whose influence boded good or evil. Non-indigenous religions—Christianity, Islam, Hinduism—eventually won converts in the islands, but, historians note, none of them ever took the place of the spirit world in the minds and hearts of indigenous tribesmen.

Chapter 4

Spirits and Ancestors

For indigenous tribes of Indonesia, the world was alive on two levels. There was the physical world of rocks, trees, animals, and people that one could see and then the world that one could not see: the world of spirits and the souls of the dead.

The spirit world remained a powerful one in the minds of tribesmen. Spirits, immortal beings who could live almost anywhere, even in trees and boats, impacted the lives of humans for good or for bad, they believed; thus it was important to maintain a good relationship with spirits at all times. Even the burial of a loved one had to be conducted in a proper manner so that he or she would be welcomed into the next world.

Early in their history Indonesians were influenced by the religious beliefs of outsiders who came to trade with them. Indian traders brought Hinduism and Buddhism to the islands; Arab traders brought Islam; Europeans, namely the Dutch and Portuguese, introduced Christianity.

Of the four, Islam achieved the greatest number of converts. Modern-day Indonesia is overwhelmingly Muslim, despite the pockets of Christianity in Kalimantan; Papua, New Guinea; Sumatra, and elsewhere. However, as author Charles Corn writes, traditional tribal beliefs still persist in the islands, even among the Muslim population:

Regardless of whatever faith—Hindu, Islam, Christian—had been imported [to the islands] it remained a veneer superimposed upon ancient animistic cultures.[25]

Protecting Women and Children

The Balinese believed that evil spirits, known as *leyaks,* brought sickness and death upon a village. *Leyaks* were shape-changers who could take almost any form—animals, fire, or a beautiful young girl. *Leyaks'* favorite food was the internal organs of children, Balinese believed. Historians say this belief dated back to ancient times, when the infant mortality rate was very high. More than likely, young children died from famine and disease. However, Balinese tradition blamed the *leyak,* who could kill an infant without leaving a mark.

Both children and pregnant women were vulnerable to the influence of evil spirits, tribesmen believed. A pregnant Dayak

An Indonesian boy poses with his dugout canoe on the shore of a river. Indigenous tribes believed in the existence of both the physical world and a world of spirits and souls.

woman and her husband observed a series of rituals that they believed would protect her and their unborn child. For example, since in Dayak society spitting was a sign of respect for the spirits, a Dayak father-to-be spent much of his time spitting about the longhouse. The pregnant woman was barred from a host of everyday tasks because, the tribe believed, her condition made the evil spirits jealous and they would do what they could do to harm her baby. The woman could not cut wood, or her child might be born with a harelip. She could not cut the limbs off an animal, or the child might be born with stumps instead of arms and legs. And she never tied a garment around her neck during pregnancy, because to do so meant the child would be born with the umbilical cord wrapped around its neck.

A Mentawai husband had many rules to follow when his wife was pregnant. For example, he could not make a dugout canoe before the baby was born. If a prospective father did make a canoe, others feared that the spirit of the tree would take its vengeance on him and his family: He might fall ill, the canoe might sink, or his wife might lose the child.

Spirits of the Field

Rice farmers, such as the Javanese and Balinese, believed that spirits lived within their crop and that the rice was to be tended and harvested in a specific fashion, so as not to offend those spirits. While harvesting the rice, tribal women brought special knives with them to the fields. The knives were curved in such a way that they could be held, almost hidden, in their palms. If the spirits could not see the knives, tribesmen believed, they would not be offended by the harvest.

The Balinese believed not only in immortal spirits but in a pantheon of gods and goddesses that governed heaven and Earth. One of their more important goddesses oversaw agriculture and fertility. During growing season tribesmen would weave an image of the goddess from rice straw and place it in the fields as a tribute to her.

Spirits of the Hunt

All living things, including fish and game, were inhabited by spirits, tribesmen believed. Thus a tribal hunt or fishing expedition had to be conducted in the proper fashion, so as not to offend those spirits. Before a hunt, tribesmen had to offer them gifts—sago, coconuts, plants, and fish—or misfortune could befall them or their families. And when they returned with meat, their families would thank the spirits of the animals before eating their meal.

The Lamalera, who are whale hunters, also pursue their quarry in a manner calculated to avoid offending the animal's spirit. When a whale is sighted, the hunters must pause in their voyage, take off their hats, and pray, "Bless our hunt and let us return alive."[26] Respecting the whale's spirit does not end when the animal is harpooned and towed to shore. Its meat and fat must all be used—every bit of it. It is an offense to the

A Balinese Festival

According to Balinese tradition, the festival of Eka Dasa Rudra should be held once every hundred years or during very difficult times. Hard times are caused by an upset in the balance between good and evil due to evil and sinful acts by man, the Balinese believe. Only prayers and sacrifices to the gods can put things right again.

Almost thirty ceremonies in all are performed during the eleven-week festival. Festivalgoers hang holy cookies on a wooden frame to symbolize a cosmos crowded with gods. Balinese legends and fairy tales are reenacted in festival dances. Images of the gods are taken in a three-day procession to the sea, where they will be symbolically washed. Finally, a water buffalo calf is sacrificed to the sea demons: Villagers tip its horns with gold, put silver bracelets on its legs, tie a stone around its neck, and push it into the sea.

Male dancers dress in saffron robes and peaked white headdresses to perform the traditional warrior dances. A barong, a mythical being believed to have defended humanity against evil, is built out of natural materials: a mane of torch ginger and rice stalks, horns made from corn and cassava, and a tail made of coconut, bananas, and bamboo. Festivalgoers make a special procession to the temple at Mount Agung, Bali's sacred mountain, and leave the barong beneath a canopy; there it will stay, they believe, to protect Bali against evil.

The festival will reach its climax when the priests offer gifts and sacrifices to Rudra, the Balinese version of the devil.

whale's spirit, tribesmen believe, to waste any part of its body.

The ill-advised sale, a generation ago, of a whale's skull is blamed for the drastic reduction in the annual harvest, a researcher learned when he visited the Lamalera in 2001. The tribe had killed fifty-six whales in 1969, tribesmen said. But that same year a whale's skull was sold to tourists. This so offended the whale's spirit, they said, that, since then, catches have rarely topped ten whales a season.

A spirit's displeasure can have even more devastating consequences for a village, and animal sacrifice may be the way a village chooses to appease the offended spirit. On the island of Flores, villagers would kill a water buffalo in a cruel and gruesome manner. To the Flores villagers, however, the buffalo symbolized whatever wrongs they had committed against each other or the spirits. Destroying it was a way of wiping out their sins. Two *National Geographic* writers elaborate:

The people want a scapegoat something to suffer for their breaches of [tribal custom, and other wrongdoings] so that sicknesses or plagues won't come to the village. They tie a buffalo in this open arena and throw spears and knives at it until it [is] wild with pain and fear, until it bleeds to death.[27]

Linking This World and the Next

Tribal shamans, or holy men, are members of the tribe who communicate directly with spirits. This role was extremely important to the tribe, but shamans also performed other important tasks within the community. The tribal shaman usually served as a physician, using his knowledge of medicinal plants to treat everything from stomachaches to burns and broken bones.

In some tribes, shamans were also called upon to "see" into the future. Mentawai shamans had a unique way of foretelling future events: They butchered a chicken or pig and examined the veins in the animal's stomach. If the veins were arranged in a particular manner, the family in question would enjoy good health and successful hunts. But if the veins were arranged in another manner, the family would be cursed with illness and unsuccessful hunts.

Shamans communicated with the spirit world through elaborate ceremonies, ritual dances, and incantations. Tribesmen believed that these ceremonies allowed the shamans to enter the kind of mental state during which

spirits talked to them. One longtime researcher describes the rituals performed during a Mentawai shaman ceremony:

> During ceremonies dancing is their vehicle to enter the spirit world. Following the rhythm of bamboo and python snake skin drums and belts, the [shamans] perform below the hanging skulls of monkeys and boars. . . . In this highly charged atmosphere some of the dancers enter a trance, a spiritual communication transporting them to a different world.[28]

Fearing the Dead

Shamans also communicated with the dead, a necessary act because the dead were not always friendly to the living, particularly if the deceased in question had been wronged by a relative. The victim, tribesmen believed, would haunt the relative and cause him mischief until the ghost's survivor made a peace offering or somehow convinced the wronged party to rest at peace.

The Asmat in particular were very fearful of vengeful ghosts and devised a system of keeping them at bay. When a relative or spouse died, his loved ones kept his skull in the house with them. As long as the skull was there, they believed, the dead person's ghost would not bother them.

Similarly, the Mentawai, who called the spirits of their dead the Ukkui, held special mass ceremonies for all the tribal dead to appease whatever anger against the living

A Dayak shaman performs a ceremonial dance. Indigenous peoples believed that tribal shamans had the ability to see into the future and to communicate with spirits.

they may have taken with them into the next world. During these rituals the tribe's shamans summoned the Ukkui by putting out whatever possessions the dead persons had owned in life: beds, fabrics, bells. The tribe then asked forgiveness for whatever wrongs had been committed against them while they were alive:

> [The shaman] are seized by spasmodic fits, their eyes rolled back, their bodies sweating and shaking vigorously. The others jump in to calm the religious fervor. A burden seems to have been lifted [from the tribe, meaning that the deceased's spirits are pleased]. The private items are stowed away and dancing soon flows.[29]

Funeral Rites

The Javanese tried to keep their dead happy in the next world by giving them the right kind of burial. They would bury the deceased's weapons and other prized possessions with him so he could use them in the next world. A funeral was extremely important to almost every indigenous tribe in the islands. However, funeral rites themselves varied widely from tribe to tribe.

Some tribes buried their dead in the ground, others left corpses in the open to decay, and some preferred cremation. Funeral practices even varied within a particular tribe depending on the age of the person who had died. Deceased Tanahmerah children, for example, were buried in the ground in bamboo boxes. A

deceased Tanahmerah adult was laid to rest in his canoe. The craft was raised about twenty-five feet in the air, and the remains were left to the elements.

The Asmat, too, placed their dead on an open platform in the jungle. The Dayak set corpses on boats known as *prahus* and set them adrift on the river, downwind from the village. The grieving tribe then gave a feast, complete with roasted pig and palm wine, in the deceased's memory.

The Balinese believed that only cremation set the soul free from the body. As with most aspects of Balinese culture, cremation ceremonies were elaborate, festive affairs: The Balinese believed that the afterworld is much like Bali itself and therefore nothing to fear. Cremation "towers," tall, pillarlike structures, were built for the ceremony. These towers were beautifully decorated with glass, colored paper, and other ornaments that doubled as kindling. The tower and the deceased's wooden coffin were carried to the cremation site by mourners, who shouted along the route to frighten away evil spirits. The tower was placed atop the coffin, which was carved to look like a bull. The fire was lit, and the tall tower generated enough heat and flames to effect cremation. After the body had burned, the remains were scooped up by hand, taken to the ocean, and spread upon the water as a final act to free the spirit.

The Toraja were also known for jolly, celebratory funerals. These rites were often delayed for some time after death so that all family members and relatives could attend and the deceased's rice fields, buffalo, and possessions could be properly disposed of. The body, which decayed slowly in the hot, humid weather, would be kept in a small building until everything was ready. On the

The body of a deceased Balinese man burns inside a wooden Brahma bull during a traditional cremation ceremony. The Balinese believed that cremation set the soul free.

day of the funeral, gongs were played, and mourners marched to the body's keeping place. The corpse was taken to its grave: a tomb carved into the side of the cliff. The family brought a large, life-size wooden likeness of the deceased, dressed in his clothes, to place before his tomb as a grave marker. The tribe also slaughtered water buffalo so the deceased would have livestock waiting for him in the afterlife. Following the interment, family and friends feasted on palm wine and roast pig.

The Afterlife

Most indigenous tribes did not believe in a heaven and hell, as in the Judeo-Christian tradition. Most believed that life after death was fairly peaceful, save for tribes like the Kombai and Korowai who had a much starker view of the hereafter. Living humans, they believed, existed in what they called the inner zone, while the dead inhabited a shadowy place known as the outer zone. Beyond both zones existed a great sea. When the world ended, the sea would flood the inner and outer zones and both the living and dead would drown.

The Asmat view of the afterworld also involved water

Deer gather on the shore of a river near a dense jungle. Some tribes believed that the dead lived in forests together with the spirits.

but in a much more benign fashion. The tribe lives in swampy areas near the south central coast of Papua, and so they spend their lives on or near water. Traditionally, the Asmat believed that the water's surface divided the worlds of the living and dead.

One could look into the water and see a look-alike ancestor staring back. Thus, the world of the dead looked much like that of the living, they concluded.

The residents of Flores believed that the dead went to live in one of three island

Borobodur

One of the great architectural wonders of Southeast Asia, the Borobodur, still stands in Java. The Borobodur is dedicated to the worship of the Buddha and was built by the region's ruling family, the Saliendras, between 778 and 824. This remarkable structure, carved out of a hillside, contains nine terraces that represent the nine previous lives of Gautama before he attained Buddhahood.

The terraces are surrounded by galleries that measure about three miles. Altogether the galleries are adorned with nearly two thousand finely detailed bas-relief sculptures, including four hundred images of the Buddha himself. The Javanese culture, as well as others in Indonesia, was deeply influenced by the Indian traders and religious advisers who visited the region over many centuries. It was these traders who introduced Hinduism and Buddhism to Indonesia. However, the Borobodur was built by the Javanese people, and their influence does appear in its image. Certain Borobodur sculptures, for example, depict Javanese scenes: princes, peasants, carpenters, potterymakers, weavers, and fishermen at work.

The temple was originally meant to serve as a repository for the soul and ashes of King Indra, during whose reign most of the construction work had taken place. For some unknown reason, Indra's ashes were never interred there. However, Borobodur drew many visitors during ancient times, and apparently many of them took away "souvenirs" the way modern tourists might. Miniature clay statues and tablets stamped with Buddha images have been dug up near Borobodur. Historians believe they may have been made by the women potters depicted in a wall carving on the temple. The potters in this carving are smoothing clay with a tool while men bring them fresh supplies.

lakes, all of which formed centuries ago in the craters of extinct volcanoes. The water in these lakes, located side by side, are colored differently due to the separate soils and minerals in each. The lake with red water was home to the souls of sorcerers and evil men. Those who died young went to the lake with green water, and everyone else went to the blue lake.

The Mentawai believed that deceased members of the tribe lived in the forest along with the spirits. They also believed their own souls could easily interact with the dead while they slept. The soul goes wandering outside the body, they believed, and these wanderings become dreams. There is always a danger that the soul will not return from its travels and the person will die in his sleep. The best way to keep the soul from wandering for good is to live a good and virtuous life, the Mentawai believed.

Outsiders Arrive

Indigenous tribesmen may have converted to Hinduism and Buddhism, the first of the major religions to arrive in the region, perhaps as early as A.D. 300, when Indian and Chinese traders began to visit the islands with regularity. Indian traders in particular had a huge impact on island society, bringing traditional cultural practices, political ideas, and their written language, Sanskrit, as well as religion. Mass conversions occurred at the highest levels, with Indonesia's ruling families embracing both faiths.

Islam made its appearance in Indonesia around A.D. 758, brought by Arab traders. By the fourteenth and fifteenth centuries the Muslim faith had spread throughout the islands; however, when the next wave of trading ships arrived from Europe, this same level of conversion did not happen.

Europeans' faith, Christianity, was considered the religion of conquerors, since Portuguese, Dutch, and English traders from the beginning sought to establish a permanent presence in the region. Arabs, Indians, and Chinese sought cultural and commercial exchanges but except for small Chinese communities that grew up on the islands, these traders had little interest in becoming settlers.

Moreover, few Christian missionaries made the treacherous voyage from Europe during the earliest years of occupation. Those who did often carried a paternalistic and condescending attitude toward the locals. The Jesuit priest Francis Xavier labored mightily to convert tribesmen despite his obvious dislike of them and their lands. He traveled through what was then called the Spice Islands and unhappily reported that he was nearly eaten alive by insects wherever he went. Yet Xavier was convinced Indonesians needed saving and wrote to colleagues in 1546 asking for their help and support:

> Immediately on arrival I visited the villages and baptized a large number of children who had not received the sacrament. . . . I give you this account so that you may see how sorely you are needed in these parts.[30]

But Xavier would enjoy precious little company in the islands. The Portuguese were soon supplanted by the Dutch, who were businessmen, not evangelists. Their only spiritual requirement would be that those tribesmen who had converted to Catholicism become Protestants, since Holland was a Protestant country.

Headhunters Convert

Christian missionaries have had the most success in remote areas where tribesmen largely went uncontacted by outsiders during the early years of foreign trade. The Batak were one such tribe: They were under pressure from nearby Muslim tribes to convert to Islam, yet they refused to do so. But in 1862 a Lutheran minister named Ludwig Nommensen came to live among them, and, with a quiet approach, over a period of decades he converted them to Christianity. The tribe eventually became so devout that it gave up the practice of cannibalism.

The head-hunting Nias of Sumatra also gave up their warring ways when Catholic and Protestant missionaries arrived in their homeland in the late 1940s. A female researcher visiting the Nias in 1961 had a frightening encounter with one of their men.

The man, brandishing a sword, shield, and spear, danced a dance around her. He then proudly presented his weapons and asked if she would like to buy them. "You like to buy my weapons? I don't need them now, I'm a Christian,"[31] he said.

Catholic missionaries arrived in Papua in the late 1950s. The Crosiers, an order based in Minnesota, have enjoyed particular success with the Asmat. These priests adapt Catholic ritual to Asmat tradition, holding mass in the tribal longhouses, building altars from tree trunks, and wear-

The Boats of Lamalera

Most indigenous tribesmen believe that inanimate objects, like rocks and houses, have souls. For the Lamalera tribe of Lembata, the most important "living" objects in their lives are their boats.

The whale-hunting Lamalerans believe that every boat they build has a soul. If a boat should fall apart of old age or break apart during a whale hunt, then that boat has "died." Villagers will mourn a "dead" boat for two months, the length of time it usually takes to build a new vessel. The construction of a Lamaleran boat always follows ancient traditions and is done by *ata molas,* highly skilled craftsmen from the tribe's boat-building clans. In the Lamaleran language *ata mola* also means priest.

Ata molas require eighteen trees to build one boat. The stern is built from the trees' roots so that the life force within them will flow to the head of the boat. Sacred symbols are painted on the prow of the boat, usually a pair of eyes, so that the boat can search for prey.

Whaling boats play an important part in Lamaleran legends and in the tribe's oral history. Tribesmen believe that their ancestors once lived on an island far to the north but that the island was destroyed by a tidal wave. The island's survivors crowded into two boats and traveled to the island of Lembata. One of the tribe's most powerful, sacred symbols is a snake coiling around a mountain: This represents the tidal wave that destroyed the tribe's ancestral home.

ing Asmat tooth necklaces and fur headbands while they say mass.

Ancient Traditions Go On

Despite efforts of nineteenth-century and contemporary Christian missionaries, Indonesia remains a Muslim nation. Eighty-seven percent of the population was Muslim in 2003, making Indonesia the largest Islamic nation in the world. Only 9 percent of the population is Christian, and Bali has remained Hindu. Yet traditional tribal beliefs are still widespread, even as Indonesians practice more conventional faiths.

The Lamalera are among the tribes who seamlessly combine old and new ways. The whale, their chief prey, is still considered sacred, and whaling crews still call upon its spirit as they hunt. But Catholic missionaries have made many converts since the 1800s and today; when whalers prepare for hunting season in May, local priests bless their fleet of boats before the season begins.

When East Meets West

New ideas, cultural practices, and religious beliefs came to Indonesia with each new wave of foreign traders. However, European traders were unlike their predecessors; they wanted to possess the Indonesian islands and their people and resources and so control the people who lived in them. Their presence in the islands would change forever the lives of indigenous tribesmen politically, culturally, and environmentally.

Chapter 5

Masters and Freedom Fighters

First the Portuguese, then the Dutch, and, briefly, the English strove to conquer the islands, subdue their most powerful rulers, and gain control of the lucrative spice trade. The Dutch, who ruled Indonesia for 350 years, established a plantation system that virtually enslaved whole populations, brought a military presence to quell frequent uprisings, and tried to force Western ideas and values onto the indigenous population.

But the Second World War disrupted Holland's drive to become a colonial power. The Japanese conquered and held the Indonesian islands for several years, and during their tenure a burgeoning independence movement gained strength. By the time the Allies defeated Japan in 1945, the leaders of this movement were ready to declare Indonesia a sovereign country. The road to independence would nonetheless be a rocky one; the Dutch would battle for years to keep Indonesia as their territory. Yet with the help and support of the United Nations, Indonesia took its first steps as a republic in the late 1940s.

The Portuguese

Like others before them, the Portuguese sailed to Indonesia in search of spices. And, like the others, they dreamed of riches. Portuguese explorer Vasco da Gama returned to Lisbon in 1499 with a cargo of spices that paid for his expedition sixty times over. Portuguese traders who followed him brought back valuable Sumatran pepper that fetched forty times its original price. Soon ship captains loaded their vessels with nutmeg and cloves, accepting help from island residents whom they described as polite and eager to trade.

But this relationship soured quickly enough, as the Portuguese began to regard their new trade partners with disdain. The view of Portuguese historian João de Barros is fairly typical of the early sixteenth century:

The people [of Indonesia] are of a tawny complexion, have lank hair, are strong-limbed and addicted to war. In everything but war they are slothful; and if there be any industry among them in agriculture or trade, it is confined to the women. . . . Altogether they are a lascivious people, false and ungrateful, but expert in learning anything. . . . Finally, these islands, according to the account given by our people, are a warren of every evil, and contain nothing good but their [spice] tree.[32]

Like the other Europeans that followed them, Portuguese officials regarded Indonesians as savages and the islands' riches theirs for the taking. Attempting to seize control of the trade routes, they attacked the city of Malacca in 1511, built a fort there, and then moved to the Spice Islands, where they established themselves in Ambon, located west of Ternate and Tidore.

But Portugal stayed on the defensive through most of its 130 years in the archipelago. Internal strife and civil war helped do them in: When Portuguese officials signed a

treaty with Ternate, neighboring Tidore, that island's rival, was so furious that Portugal had to gingerly side-step ensuing hostilities. The powerful ruling family of Aceh, a

Portuguese explorer Vasco da Gama brought Indonesian spices back to Portugal in 1499.

Muslim sultanate, despised the Portuguese for their Christianity and frequently tried to interfere in Portugal's shipping.

Religion was the downfall of the Portuguese in many ways. Portuguese captains often used the excuse of a "holy war" to attack Muslim ships, though the locals regarded these attacks as acts of piracy. And the Portuguese sailors themselves made poor missionaries, as author D.R. Sardesai notes in his book, *Southeast Asia Past and Present*. The boorish behavior of these traders, he suggests, may have made Islam even more popular among the native population. Sardesai writes:

> Conversion to Christianity was very marginal. Instead, by trying to force Christianity on the people of the region the Portuguese inadvertently glamorized Islam as a weapon against Portuguese oppression. The rapid spread of Islam [in the region] in the sixteenth century could be counted among Portugal's indirect, and indeed, unintended cultural contributions to the region.[33]

In retrospect, Portuguese influence was limited and fairly brief. They would be replaced by the Dutch in 1641, when Holland captured Malacca.

The Dutch Arrive

Dutch influence in Indonesia was powerful or negligible, depending on what part of the region is being discussed. Dutch traders, and later colonists and officials, would leave a mark upon the coastal trading communities and on the rice valleys of Java, which under their guidance were slowly transformed into sugar and coffee plantations. But the tribes of the remote rain forests lived undisturbed for years. The Asmat had little contact with the Dutch until Holland established a colonial outpost in Papua during the 1930s. The Kombai and Korowai remained isolated until the 1960s, when Christian missionaries befriended them.

"In Eastern Indonesia the Dutch destroyed a traditional way of life, decimated the population and adversely affected the living standards of the survivors," Zainu'ddin writes. "In the west they [the Moluccas, Sulawesi, and Papua] barely made any impact at all, except perhaps in the immediate vicinity of their trading posts."[34]

Spices had lured the Dutch, just as it had the Portuguese. But Holland's plans were much more ambitious; in time they would control the region's trade routes and press local tribesmen to grow nonindigenous crops, like cotton, coffee, and indigo, instead of rice.

Holland's strong navy and superior firepower pushed swiftly through the islands. They set up operations in Banda, Java, and Ternate and pushed English traders out of Sulawesi in 1667. They survived several skirmishes with the Javanese kingdoms and by 1694 controlled nearly all of Java.

In Sumatra they took advantage of internal strife to override its powerful sultanates. They found the ruler of the Minangkabau in a precarious position: He had delegated so much authority to village chiefs that they had begun to ignore him. These chiefs eagerly traded with the Dutch and, when their ruler tried to take revenge, sought protection from them. The Batak tribes of Sumatra were chafing under incursions from Aceh to the north and Minangkabau to the south, both of which were Muslim. The Batak signed peace treaties with the Dutch, hoping for protection.

Dutch incursions into Sumatra had little impact on the day-to-day lives of the inland peoples. Dutch officials and traders tended to work only along the coastal regions, where the sultanates were likely to fight back. Moreover, British adventurers had begun to make inroads into western Sumatra. Through

A steam locomotive loaded with sugarcane passes a young rice farmer. The Dutch established vast sugar plantations on the island of Java.

A Javanese worker inspects a vine for ripe coffee beans. The Dutch introduced coffee growing to Java during the eighteenth century.

the seventeenth and eighteenth centuries, Holland would have to share that island with England.

But the Dutch had Java all to themselves. They built a settlement, Batavia, and introduced coffee growing to Java in the early eighteenth century. They built sugar plantations—sugar had always grown naturally on Java but had never been processed or exported—and grew cotton and indigo. This new plantation system swallowed up land that ordinarily would have been used for growing rice. The Dutch had also disrupted village life, setting in place a system of government whereby the indigenous chiefs served as intermediaries between the people and Dutch officials. The selection of chiefs friendly to Dutch plans was always greatly encouraged.

Early Conflicts

Holland's relations with tribesmen outside the ranks of the leadership throughout the islands soured early on. In 1680 a British ship and crew stopped at the island of Bangka, home to a Dutch settlement and fort, as the guest of its Dutch governor. The ship's captain sat down at a table set with silver dishes and punch bowl, ready to enjoy a lavish dinner with the governor, but then their evening was interrupted:

> One of the soldiers cried out, "[natives]," and spoil'd the entertainment; for immediately the governor, without speaking one word, leapt out of one of the windows, to get as soon as he could to the fort.

A Slave Rebels

The Dutch had to quash many rebellions during their long colonial rule of Indonesia, but one of the earliest of these uprisings occurred not far from their settlement, Batavia, and was led by a runaway slave.

Early in the eighteenth century, a slave named Surapati fled his Javanese masters and set up a camp in the mountains south of Batavia where he organized a rebellion against the Dutch among the local tribesmen. Dutch officials sent soldiers to capture him, but Surapati successfully sought refuge in the court of Amangkurat III, in the latter's kingdom in east Java. Surapati settled near his benefactor and began to carve out a kingdom for himself in the Mataram region of east Java.

The Dutch were highly displeased with Amangkurat for harboring Surapati, and they decided to take down the king along with the slave. They made it known that they supported Amangkurat's uncle, Pangeran Puger, as the rightful king. Puger attacked his nephew, and the ensuing conflict became known as the first Javanese War of Succession.

Puger won the conflict with Dutch help and deposed his nephew. In return he signed a treaty with Holland that was very favorable to the Europeans. Amangkurat, meanwhile, had taken refuge with Surapati in East Java. But the Dutch were not through with these rivals and came after them both. By 1706 Surapati had been killed in battle and Amangkurat had fled the island. However, Surapati's followers would fight on; it was not until 1772 that the Dutch were finally able to subdue them.

He was followed by his officers and servants. . . . A . . . canoe full of armed [natives] had set on [nearby] Dutch soldiers catching . . . fish for the banquet.[35]

Holland's troubles in the Spice Islands stemmed from Dutch officials' refusal to respect the way islanders preferred to do business. Asian and Arab merchants had long been acclimated to the casual ways of the islands. Spice Islanders liked to do business at leisure and even to change their minds if the situation called for it. The Dutch, however, believed that a bargain was a bargain, and if the islanders happened to change their minds, the Dutch would get angry. These outbursts of temper had not endeared them to the locals.

Holland's land grabs had outraged the Javanese in central and east Java, and these tribesmen reacted violently. The Dutch often found themselves quashing uprisings by the Javanese. Then, too, they became embroiled in Java's internal struggles. Despite the Dutch presence on the island, Java's ruling families had retained some power, and these rulers continued to battle one another for land and supremacy. Dutch settlers and traders often found themselves caught in the middle when disagreements flared between these local monarchs.

A British Interlude, a Dutch Return

The British made their first appearance in the archipelago in 1579, when Sir Francis Drake landed on the island of Ternate. Ternate's sultan, Baab, welcomed Drake with open arms; in his mind the Dutch had already worn out their welcome. Twenty-four years later England claimed the island of Pulau Run, only two and a half miles long, but chock-full of nutmeg trees.

The Dutch resisted Britain's presence in the islands until the early nineteenth century, when Napoleon began his march across Europe. With Holland overrun with French troops in 1795, the Dutch king, William V, fled to London. He authorized his British protectors to take over Dutch interests in Indonesia. England occupied Java for three years, beginning in 1811. In 1814 England returned Java to Holland. But it would not be a happy homecoming for the Dutch. Beginning in the 1820s they faced a series of revolts in Borneo, Sulawesi, and western Sumatra, all violent uprisings that put a drain on Dutch finances. During the same decade Diponegoro, son of a Javanese king, led a revolt against the Dutch. By the time he was captured in 1830, Java had been devastated by war. Nearly fifteen thousand Dutch troops and two hundred thousand Javanese had been killed.

The Dutch Expand Their Empire

Once Javanese resistance had been quelled, Holland instituted an even tougher plantations system. Javanese were forced to build bridges and roads and to act as servants to Dutch officials. The Dutch were also experimenting with new crops, such as tobacco. The demand for

Two emaciated Javanese women wait for food at a Dutch relief agency. Because Dutch colonists primarily cultivated crops such as coffee and tobacco, insufficient food was grown to feed the indigenous population.

export crops had become so great that the locals had little room left for rice. By the 1840s the Javanese population had experienced several famines. But business was going so well for the Dutch that they decided to expand their interests elsewhere in the Indonesian islands. Tribes in Sumatra and Sulawesi had recently converted to Christianity and did not protest a Dutch presence in their territory. The Muslim Acehnese, however, continued to resist, and in 1873, Holland attacked Aceh. Aceh's sultan fell quickly, but his supporters kept up a guerrilla war that lasted years. Bali and Lombok had heretofore remained independent of Dutch rule, but Holland's military might continued to press against them, and by the early twentieth century, both islands were Dutch possessions.

Attempts to Make Amends

Thanks in part to its island empire, Holland had grown quite wealthy. However, as the new century dawned, a growing number of Hollanders voiced concern over the plight of island residents, most of whom still struggled with hunger and poverty. In response the Dutch government enacted what was known as Holland's Ethical Policy in 1901. This policy was meant to expand health programs on the islands, change agricultural policies, and transfer power to local officials. The policy, officials said, would free up land for rice growing. It would establish village banks offering low-cost loans that would in turn help villagers purchase land. The Dutch

would open schools, too, for the indigenous children.

But this well-intentioned policy ended up mostly benefiting the region's wealthiest and most powerful indigenous families. They alone had the monies to quickly buy up the land that had suddenly become available. They also took advantage of Dutch schooling in ways that poorer families could not. Each village would have a school, the Dutch said, but villagers would build the schools themselves and pay fees to send their sons—almost never their daughters, since education for women would not become acceptable until later—to school. Many schools were built, and parents often made incredible sacrifices to send children there. Sadly, though, Dutch education often had the effect of estranging a child from parents and village alike. Once a youth finished his education, he would leave home, often for good, to seek a job in the urban areas.

This exodus from villages to the cities was a development that Dutch officials had hoped for. Dutch government and business interests had grown on the islands, and officials required a pool of educated indigenous workers to fill lower-level jobs. Moreover, education the Dutch arranged for was an effective counter to Islamic schools, which had been the only education available to island youngsters. The Christian Dutch, who had so long clashed with the followers of Islam, wished to discourage Muslim influence in Indonesia as much as possible.

Zainu'ddin writes that in the end Holland's Ethical Policy may have hurt more than it helped:

> The Dutch regarded the villagers as children whom they sought to help. They gave them what they felt they ought to want, whether they wanted it or not.[36]

The Birth of Nationalism

But Indonesia's burgeoning educated class had a far different impact than the Dutch imagined. This new class of islanders realized that although they made far less in wages than the Dutch, their duties and abilities were similar. These educated tribesmen, who had begun to think of themselves as Indonesians, took an interest in their own histories and culture. At first the Dutch paid little attention to what they regarded as a small, disgruntled minority. But over a thirty-seven-year period, this movement grew. During the 1920s those interested in nationalism formed study groups; by exchanging ideas and information, they hoped to give their countrymen a taste of future responsibilities and prepare for independence from Holland. Indonesia's first president, Sukarno—who, like other Indonesians, did not have a last name—founded one of these study clubs.

Indonesian statesman Sukarno became the country's first president in 1945.

The Slaughter of the Bandanese

The Bandanese are the indigenous peoples of the Banda Islands and for centuries they cultivated valuable groves of nutmeg trees. Nutmeg grew naturally on the islands, thanks to the birds that ate the meat of nutmeg fruit and scattered its seeds, but the Bandanese had learned long ago that nutmeg and another spice extracted from the tree, mace, was greatly valued by outsiders, and thus they took care to cultivate their own trees. The Bandanese had a fleet of large ships and traded nutmeg and mace to Asian, Arab, and Javanese traders for tools, rice, and other goods. They became one of the great trading fraternities of the southern Moluccas and thus stood in the way of total Dutch control of the spice trade. The Dutch, who were pursuing their interests elsewhere in the islands, wished to end the Bandanese monopoly on nutmeg. They provoked the Bandanese into doing battle with them and the results were disastrous.

The majority of the Bandanese were slaughtered, and many were decapitated or hanged. The Dutch even paid a group of Japanese samurai to come into the Bandas and fight and perform executions. Of the original fifteen thousand Bandanese, only six hundred survived. Their descendants still live on the Bandas, and while some grow nutmeg, others have moved on to more modern pursuits, such as providing support services to scuba divers who visit the islands.

The fruit of the nutmeg tree has lured traders to Indonesia for centuries.

The nationalists took the extraordinary step of declaring a national language for a country, which technically did not even exist. This language would be called Indonesian and would be a form of Malay, which was already spoken on the west coast of Sumatra. Indonesia's various peoples had spoken their own languages for so long that national identity could only come about if the islands were united by a common language, the nationalists felt. Sukarno and his colleagues rejected the Javanese language, despite its widespread use, because of its close association with the Dutch. The official language of Indonesia was adopted at the Second Congress of Indonesian Youth in 1928, and despite its lack of recognition by the Dutch, the nationalists began to publish a journal written entirely in Indonesian.

Alarmed by this show of independence, the Dutch cracked down. They forbade the terms Indonesia and Indonesian—the islands were then formally called the Dutch East Indies—and the flying of the newly adopted Indonesian flag. However, outside forces would alter the fate of both countries. War broke out in 1939, Germany conquered Holland, and Japanese forces landed in the islands in 1942.

The Japanese in Indonesia

At first, Indonesians greeted the Japanese as liberators. Remarked an Indonesian nationalist, "For the average Indonesian, the war . . . was simply a struggle in which the Dutch colonial rulers finally would be punished by Providence for the evil, the arrogance and the oppression they had brought to Indonesia."[37]

However, islanders soon learned that the Japanese were no better than their predecessors. In fact, Japan would rule with a cruel and iron hand, exporting Indonesians to other occupied territories where cheap labor was needed. Roughly 270,000 Indonesian men, most of them Javanese, were taken by force from their homes during the war. In some areas, whole villages of able-bodied men were taken, leaving only women, children, and old men behind. Only seventy-thousand of these men were ever found after the war.

But inadvertently the Japanese would encourage Indonesia's drive towards independence. Physical strength and military training were important to Japan, so the occupiers formed military groups among Indonesia's youth and trained them for guerrilla warfare. The Japanese also demanded that radios be installed in any village that was reachable by road; these radios, ironically enough, were a lifeline that connected Indonesians to the outside world.

Pressing for Independence

Indonesia after the Japanese surrender was a different place. Its people were no longer isolated, and some of them had been trained militarily. The Dutch were ready to return, but Indonesians did not want them back, and their nationalist leaders were ready to declare independence. Sukarno, seizing the moment, read a declaration of independence in front of his residence on

Holland's Queen Wilhelmina became head of state in Indonesia in 1947 and oversaw all of the country's foreign affairs.

August 17, 1945. News of the declaration was broadcast around the world, and sympathetic observers in Britain, the United States, Holland, and Australia took up the Indonesian cause. The Committee for the Preparation of Indonesian Independence elected Sukarno as the country's first president. Writes Zainu'ddin,

> For the people themselves the first reaction was one of excitement and bewilderment. At last they were independent, but what did this mean? One lower-class revolutionary described it in later years as being rather like awakening from a deep sleep and trying to regain one's bearings.[38]

In a matter of weeks Indonesians had established a government, a civil service, and an army staffed by soldiers who had once been members of Japanese guerilla units. Treaties at the end of the war had ensured that Indonesia would be returned to the Dutch, but Indonesians continued to resist. After two years of struggle, a compromise was reached: The Dutch monarch, Queen Wilhelmina, would be head of state in Indonesia, Holland would handle foreign affairs and defense, and Indonesian officials would oversee financial and economic issues. However, the power struggle simmered.

On July 20, 1947, the Dutch engaged in a police action to restore order in Indonesia. They had, however, underestimated both local support for the nationalists and world reaction: Dock workers in Australia refused to load Indonesian ships, and a number of Asian countries refused landing rights to Dutch planes. In

August, the United Nations Security Council ordered a cease-fire.

Holland's Last Ditch Efforts

Despite world sympathy and support, the Dutch continued to press their territorial rights. Indonesia signed an agreement with Holland in January 1948, which ceded territory in Java and Sumatra to the Dutch. The fledgling nation itself was weak and beset by internal strife: Muslim and Communist factions had already engineered unrest. The Dutch decided the time was ripe to strike again; they captured

The Regent's Daughter

During the nineteenth century the daughter of a high-ranking Javanese official took a revolutionary step: She advocated opening the colony's educational system to women of her class and preserving the indigenous culture of her people. Tragically, the young woman, Kartini, died before she could make most of her dreams come true.

Many of the wealthier Javanese families were allowed to participate in colonial government. Their Dutch masters called the heads of these families regents, and Kartini was the daughter of one of these regents. Traditionally, wealthy Javanese girls stayed quietly at home and waited for their parents to find them husbands. But Kartini had been educated in a Western-style school with her brothers, and she chafed at such a traditional fate. Kartini was a voluminous reader, and she corresponded with friends in the Netherlands whom she had met in school. When Kartini was sixteen, she received her father's permission to move to Batavia. Her Dutch friends arranged to obtain a grant for her to study in Holland, but she rejected it, fearing she would become alienated from her people. Her parents arranged a marriage with the Regent of Rembang, who shared her progressive ideas. She opened a school for the daughters of regents in her home, and she and her new husband planned to encourage revival of woodcarving and other traditional crafts that were already disappearing. Kartini also hoped to publish a book of Javanese legends, but she died at the age of twenty-five, four days after giving birth to a son.

Kartini's Dutch friends preserved her letters, which outlined many progressive ideas that were later adopted by her people. The letters were later collected and published. They are considered a good description of life in a wealthy Javanese household in the late nineteenth century. The woman who wrote them is considered Indonesia's first modern intellectual and writer.

Sukarno and other leaders, created a blockade of trade goods, and cut off communication so completely that the rest of the world did not know what had happened for weeks.

However, rather than fall into Dutch hands again, islanders decided to resist. Tribesmen who had been living for years in the cities migrated back to their home territories; Batak tribesmen returned to their ancestral villages, and Minangkabau journeyed on foot across mountains and jungles, where they were in constant fear of tiger attacks, to reach their home territory in the interior. There they would be out of reach of the Dutch influence and pressure, at least for the time being.

But the United Nations stepped in again; its members were outraged by the Dutch action. In 1949 they brought Holland and Indonesia back to the bargaining table, this time at the Hague. Holland's new queen, Juliana, signed a resolution on December 27, 1949, giving full control of Indonesia to Indonesians. During the 1950s Indonesia joined the UN.

The Road to the Modern Era

The new republic of Indonesia faced a daunting challenge: building a sense of national unity for a country that had existed for thousands of years as a group of separate civilizations. The country also faced a host of political and economic problems that after several decades have yet to abate.

Chapter 6

A People at the Crossroads

The country of Indonesia was half powder keg, half land of opportunity in the beginning of the twenty-first century. Its peoples had just deposed an authoritarian ruler, Suharto, whose good works for the country had become obscured by his ruthless treatment of political opponents and relentless crackdowns on civil liberties. They were also facing widespread unemployment, ethnic tensions, religion-inspired violence, and even separatist movements: peoples in Papua, New Guinea; Aceh; and elsewhere were agitating for their own separate states. The indigenous peoples also were facing the loss of their cultural traditions and, in some cases, their land itself. Indonesia's rich and varied ecosystem also faced environmental challenges, as some scientists even predicted that its lowland rain forests would be gone in less than a decade.

Yet the bright spots of Indonesia continue to be the people themselves. The nation's tribes continue to hope for some national identity and strive to carve a place for themselves in the modern world, often by adapting traditional ways to current economic systems. It remains to be seen whether such a group of people can continue to cobble together a national identity in the face of such exacting challenges.

The Iron Hand of Government

Indonesia's efforts at maintaining a democratic government were troubled from the very start. Sukarno, the nation's first president, survived an attempt to overthrow his harsh and repressive government in 1965. A year later, however, he was stripped of his powers, and a new leader, Suharto, became acting president. Suharto led a backlash against the Indonesian Communist Party, which had existed since the 1940s. Clashes following the coup left many thousands of Indonesians dead.

Suharto instituted a number of economic changes and modernization and enticed

Lieutenant general Suharto became Indonesia's president in 1966. He ruled the country as a dictator for more than thirty years.

ble in the United States. And Suharto's government, like the Dutch government before them, hoped to expand Indonesian interests elsewhere in the region.

Suharto's predecessor, Sukarno, had negotiated for the acquisition of Papua, then known as Irian Jaya, from the Dutch after obtaining his country's freedom in the 1940s. Papua was a Dutch possession, though not officially part of the Dutch East Indies territory. The UN agreed in 1962 to allow Indonesia to administer Papua, with a vote on the issue coming seven years later. The vote, conducted on August 2, 1969, went in Indonesia's favor. However, critics charged that the one thousand tribal chieftains allowed to vote had been forced by armed supporters of the Indonesian government to vote yes.

Six years later, East Timor, a former Portuguese colony located west of Bali, was annexed by Indonesia by force, though the UN did not recognize Indonesia's right to the territory.

Both Sukarno and Suharto ruled in an authoritarian style that was ultimately incompatible with democratic government. Suharto ruled for six terms as president, but his power waned in the 1990s as financial troubles threatened to overwhelm the country. In the 1990s Indonesia's economy crashed, and

foreign investment to the islands. The country attracted oil, natural gas, and mining companies and manufacturers, like Nike, who were looking to produce their goods far less expensively than was possi-

82

Suharto's fortunes went with it. The value of Indonesia's currency plummeted, inflation soared, and unemployment skyrocketed. The International Monetary Fund stepped in, but the fixes the UN agency attempted to impose made matters worse instead of better. Suharto was elected to a seventh term in March 1998, but appointments of old cronies sparked violent demonstrations.

Suharto's resignation in 1998 gave hope to those who wished to reassert democracy in Indonesia. Yet even optimistic officials conceded that the country's problems went far beyond Suharto. Indonesia is a land where people still think of themselves in terms of regional differences. Such differences sparked separatist movements in Aceh, Papua, and East Timor. Residents of East Timor continued to resist Indonesian

The Rise and Fall of a President

Suharto, Indonesia's second president, ruled the country for thirty years and was elected to six terms, although most observers say that those elections, and his rule, were hardly democratic. He was born in 1921 to Javanese parents and after his parents' divorce spent most of his youth with relatives. He joined the Dutch army in 1940 and was promoted to sergeant. He received additional military training during the Japanese occupation and in 1945 commanded troops in a years-long effort to permanently expel the Dutch from the islands. After Indonesian independence Suharto rose through the military ranks and led operations to suppress Muslim and Communist dissenters. After Indonesia's first president, Sukarno, was stripped of his powers in 1966, Suharto was named acting president. He was elected president a year later and held that office until 1998.

Suharto took a leadership role in eco-nomic development and attracted substantial foreign investment to Indonesia. He developed roads and irrigation systems and expanded health and educational facilities and family planning programs. But Suharto won few friends with his crackdown on civil liberties, which included repression of Muslims who wanted a greater role in government, writers who demanded more artistic freedoms, and rival politicians.

The citizenry finally abandoned him in 1997 when Indonesia plunged into an economic crisis. Suharto was elected to a seventh term in March 1998, but appointments of old cronies to key posts sparked demonstrations by students and calls for democratic reforms. Police shot six students in May of the same year. Five hundred people were dead after two days of arson and looting in Jakarta. On May 21 Suharto resigned the presidency.

rule, and in 1999 the citizenry overwhelmingly voted to separate from Indonesia. After a long and bloody struggle, East Timor finally achieved independence on May 20, 2002.

The Faithful Clash with One Another

For many indigenous peoples, religion still means a great deal more than nationalism. Researcher Tim Severin, while camped in the community of Warbal on the Kei Islands, noted as much in observing the devout Christian community around him:

> The community was intensely and actively religious. When the Warbal islanders did not go to church to pray they met in one another's homes; small groups of men and women could be seen entering one of the little houses, prayer books in hand, at almost any time of day.[39]

Islam remains the dominant force in the islands, however, and Christians remain a small minority. Tensions between Christians and Muslims continue to simmer in part because of the history of conflict between the two groups that dates back to the arrival of the Europeans. Clashes between Muslims and Christians in recent years have been tragic. In 1999 the Christian community on Ternate was attacked by their Muslim neighbors. The Ternate Muslims had heard a rumor that the Christians were planning to attack them, and on that basis they executed a preemptive strike. The

rumor, as it turned out, was false, and no attack by the Christians had been planned. By then it was too late; houses, property, and, in some cases, lives had already been destroyed.

Militant Islam on the Rise

Small groups of hard-line Muslims who believe that Indonesia should be a Muslim nation that accepts neither other faiths nor Western influences have grown in number in recent years. Some of these Islamic militants are behind a separatist movement in Aceh. The Acehnese have been devoutly Muslim for centuries, and the militants among them believe that, because of this, Aceh should be a separate, Muslim nation. In 2001 reports of human rights abuses and the killings of innocent civilians after soldiers clashed with Acehnese separatists surfaced.

This kind of hard-line thinking has become popular enough in Indonesia to alarm its many peace-loving citizens. Mochtar Buchori, a member of Indonesia's parliament, is among those committed to their Muslim faith but willing to live in a nation that includes those of other faiths. Buchori believes that the growth of hard-line Islamic militancy could threaten Indonesia's future. As he explained in a 2001 *National Geographic* article, more moderate Muslim voices are being drowned out by the hard-liners:

> What kind of Islam are we going to have as the mainstream? If we're heading for a hard-line [militant]

Indonesian marines in a raft patrol the area surrounding the Exxon-Mobil plant.

Islamic civilization, this country's really going to disintegrate.[40]

Hard-line militants want no Western presence in Indonesia, and American companies doing business on the islands have suffered. In 2001 some companies became fearful enough of reprisals to their employees and interests to take action. Nike evacuated the families of its American employees as a precautionary measure that year. Other companies with Indonesian plants and interests, like Exxon-Mobil, added new guards at its plants for security reasons.

Conflict with the Chinese

Conflicts among citizens in Indonesia stem not only from religious differences. Tensions have simmered for years between the indigenous population and Indonesia's ethnic Chinese minority.

The Chinese first came to Indonesia as traders, but many decided to settle in the islands. Chinese settlers were already in place when the Dutch arrived, living as merchants and even advisers in the courts of Indonesia's kings. By the early eighteenth century there were about ten thousand Chinese living in east Java alone. They owned large parcels of lands and served as craftsmen, tea traders, and sugar farmers. By the end of that same century the Chinese community was serving as middlemen between the Javanese and the Dutch. The Javanese were at the lower end of this scale, growing crops, doing the manual labor, and getting only a small cut of the profits. The Chinese, who delivered crops to the Dutch, got a much bigger share. This arrangement fostered resentment among the indigenous peoples that has never truly disappeared. And as time wore on, the Chinese, despite being only 2.6 percent of the population, staunchly occupied the middle class, and there appeared to be little room for the indigenous peoples to move out of poverty.

When Indonesia entered a financial crisis in the late 1990s, the Chinese became scapegoats in the minds of some. In May 1998, riots erupted in the streets, and Chinese residents were the victims of the violence. Officials estimated that some 1,200 Chinese were murdered and about 150 Chinese women had been raped. Many Chinese even left the region, fearing for their lives.

Anxious to calm tensions and make amends, the government took steps to integrate Chinese culture into the mainstream. To that end, the Chinese New Year is now officially celebrated in Indonesia.

The Poor Stay Poor

Despite the investment capital flowing in from Nike, Exxon-Mobil, and other multinational corporations anxious to exploit the island's rich resources, Indonesia remains one of the world's desperately poor countries. Experts report that the gap between the rich and poor is narrower in Indonesia than in Thailand, the Philippines, or Malaysia, but this seemingly encouraging statistic illustrates, as well, that few in Indonesia have been able to acquire great wealth.

For the average Indonesian, unemployment and difficult living conditions remain the norm. The difficult economic situation has devastated rural life in particular. Many young people leave their home villages for the cities to look for work. More and more, observers say, villages tend to be populated by older people.

Young Indonesians have found, however, that moving to the outskirts of the cities is not a panacea. Johnston offers this description of a more contemporary Dayak community, far from the traditional longhouse:

The villages we passed seemed as degraded as the forest: temporary, tin-roofed shacks built by Dayaks who had migrated to the coast. . . . It was a familiar Third World Scene, and one I'd viewed often from the window seat of a bus: indigenous trying to survive on the bottom rung of capitalism; women struggling to make a home out of plastic table cloths and broken mirrors; men either unemployed or away at labor camps;

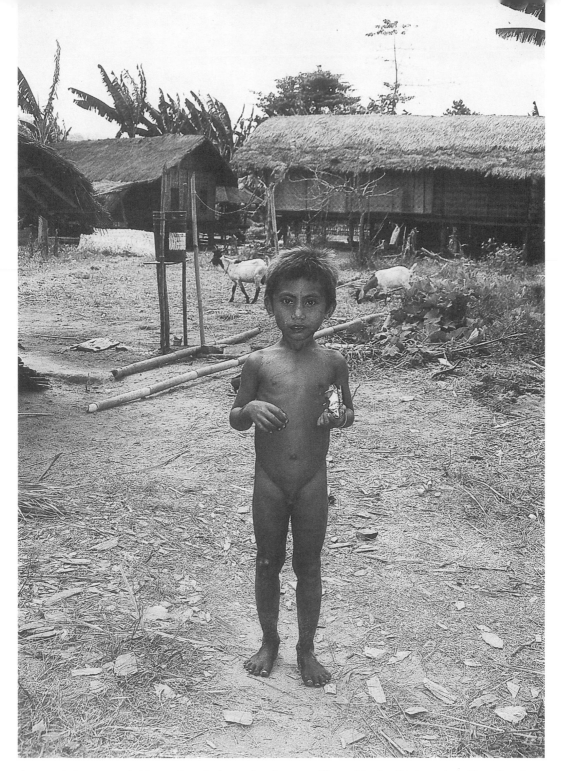

A poor Indonesian child stands naked in a Sumbawan village. Much of Indonesia still suffers from extreme poverty and unemployment.

children in hot pursuit of the products they see on television.[41]

Problems for those who live in Indonesia's urban centers go far beyond unemployment and housing, Severin notes during his trip through the Moluccas:

We had barely entered the great bay and were still ten kilometers from the modern city when we encountered a slimy yellow slick of plastic bags, old bottles and raw sewage floating out on the tide. . . . The pollution of Ambon's harbour was explained when we took a bus into the city center and saw that three or four small creeks cut through the town and emptied into the harbour. All of them were serving as main sewers.[42]

In the minds of some observers, the situation for Indonesia's indigenous peoples has gotten better, if only because they were so bad to start with. Princeton economist Paul Krugman, who often writes on issues of global trade, regards the presence of large corporations as having made a difference; at least jobs have been provided. Yet even he says that standards for more developed countries cannot be applied to Indonesia:

A country like Indonesia is still so poor that progress can be measured in terms of how much the average person gets to eat: since 1970, per capita intake has risen from less than 2,100 to more than 2,800 calories a day. A shocking one-third of young children are still malnourished—but in 1975, the fraction was more than half.[43]

Resettlement

Indonesia's economic troubles stem from many causes, but a growing population has exacerbated them. By 2003 the census had topped 234 million, with the bulk of the people living in Java, historically the region's most crowded island. Realizing that a very high concentration of people in one area makes for squalid living conditions, the government long ago decided to encourage its citizens to move elsewhere. Under the terms of a resettlement program begun in 1969, citizens were given incentives to move from Java to other areas. About 8.5 million people were relocated to Sumatra, Kalimantan, the Moluccas, and Papua between 1969 and 1994.

Resettlement, however, caused far more problems than it did successes. Most of those relocated had a difficult time adjusting and were ill equipped to deal with a new environment. Says Johnston in *Shooting the Boh,*

[New villages] had been carved out of the forest by the Indonesian government to encourage migration from the big cities: each family was issued a house, food for a year, an acre and a half of land, and enough rice to plant several crops. But the government overlooked the fact that growing rice is difficult, if not impossible, on the thin layer of soil that underlies a rainforest. And the immigrants that came from the urban slums were ill-equipped to farm in the first place. Most of them . . . ended up working for the logging companies.[44]

Local populations, observers say, were swamped by the newcomers, and few services existed to help them. Even worse, tribesmen are losing their ancestral homelands due to the resettlement. The Dayak were particularly hard hit; many families had been pushed off their land into the uninviting new settlements. The Dayak are mostly Christian, and those relocated into their homeland were the Madurese, a Muslim tribe. The Dayak accused the Madurese of taking the best of the economy for themselves: running area shops and working in the factories.

The arrival of the Muslim Madurese prompted the Dayak, who had given up their head-hunting ways after converting to Christianity, to become warriors again, as a reporter describes in this 2001 *Newsweek* article:

The Madurese were met by a large crowd of machete-swinging Dayaks. . . . The handful of police ran away, and the Dayaks descended. They beheaded some of the Madurese and ripped open chests to tear out and eat still-beating hearts.[45]

Many Dayak leaders condemned the killings, but they still despised the resettle-ment policy. Thus, in 2001, some Dayak were calling for a separate Kalimantan state.

As for resettlement itself, by 2001 it had been declared a failure and halted by the government.

Nature in Jeopardy

One of the unintended consequences of resettlement was the clearing away of rain forest to support the new villages. By the beginning of the twenty-first century, loss of rain forest had become a serious problem in Indonesia, so critical that in 2001 some scientists were predicting that Sumatra's lowland forests would disappear by 2005 and Kalimantan's forests would be destroyed by 2010.

The loss of forestland would cause incalculable damage to wildlife and people. Indonesia is home to forty thousand flowering plants, three thousand species of trees, and five thousand orchids, most of which would vanish without the rain-forest canopy. Indonesia's environment is also home to orangutans, wild oxen, black gibbon monkeys, tapirs, Sumatran tigers, cassowaries, birds of paradise, Asian elephants, and indigenous peoples such as the Asmat, Yali, and Dani.

Indonesia's forest wood—sandalwood, teak, and ramin—have always been in high demand by commercial loggers who sell Indonesian wood products overseas. However, illegal logging by small crews who cut trees and sell them without permission is the biggest threat to forestland. From 1990 to 1995 Indonesia lost an estimated 20,930 square miles of tropical forest as a result of illegal logging. The government has attempted a crackdown on the practice, but enforcement of logging regulations remains poor.

Some of this illegal cutting has been done by indigenous tribesmen anxious to make money. The Mentawai harvested aloeswood trees relentlessly in the 1990s, enjoying the extra cash they earned and buying Western-style possessions. During the same decade Asmat tribesmen sold tree trunks they harvested for $1.30 apiece and used the money to buy radios and new Western-style clothes.

Loss of Indonesian rain forest has a far-ranging impact that goes far beyond the

Armed with a rifle and a spear, a Dayak tribesman and his sons bar the entrance to the home of Madurese settlers.

islands themselves. Land clearance increases the risk of flooding and fire; and in 1998 and 1999 wildfires caused smoke that blanketed the mainland and hurt Southeast Asia's economies and health.

Preserving a Treasure

But in recent years the Indonesian government has stepped in to preserve the rain forest, if only because it has become a lure for tourists. Because Indonesia's national budget is so tight, the country has had to rely on foreign funds and the generosity of international conservation organizations to purchase land.

Still, the government has made Mount Bromo, located in east Java, part of its national park system, and Wasur National Park, covering 1 million acres of savannah, lowland forests, swamp, and beach, is almost the size of Everglades National Park in Florida.

The Baun Nature Reserve on Aru is known as the home of the birds of paradise and protects areas on the land and in the sea that are the habitats of birds of paradise, bottlenose dolphins, rare aquatic mammals called dugongs, and sea turtles. The reserve attracts enough tourists that additional monies are brought into the local town, known as Kobadanga. The area has become wealthy enough to support a downtown with shops and a paved road.

Preserving a Nation's Culture

Preserving the nation's many cultures may prove even more difficult than saving its rain forest. As early as the 1960s, Western influence had left its mark on the tribes and erased ancient traditions. As one observer who studied the Nias, former headhunters who now embrace Christianity, said,

> Lutheran missionaries introduced Christianity in the mid 20th century. Today, Nias men sing hymns instead of hunting heads. Their children go to school, and the old ways die out.[46]

Western ways are now so pervasive in the islands that in some areas only remnants of local culture remain. Whereas Toraja tribesmen built traditional houses with their intricate carved designs, they now cover them with paint and furnish them with television sets and compact disc players. Asmat children play soccer in the jungle, and other tribesmen pursue badminton, tennis, and other Western sports. Westernization has also had an impact on the way that Indonesians dress. When Severin traveled the Spice Islands, he found the appearance of islanders almost uniform:

> Much of the regional differences were gone, particularly among the more populated regions. We could see no regional differences among the visitors at Dobbo [in the Aru Islands] in either dress or features. Everyone looked and dressed much the same in cheap trousers and shirts, their hair cut short.[47]

However, some traditional art forms, like shadow puppet theater, still remain popular. Artists in Bali also pursue music and dance, to the delight of tourists. Observers also say that young Indonesians have a renewed interest in their culture. Author Charles Lindsay says this about the Mentawai people:

Today, it is the young, educated Mentawaians who have become most mindful of their ethnic roots. They defend themselves against the condescension to which their people have been exposed, and seek ways to assert Mentawaian identity within modern developments.[48]

Rangers from an elephant patrol unit in a national park search for illegal loggers. Thousands of square miles of tropical rain forest have been lost to illegal logging.

Making a Living

For some tribesmen, however, their culture has become their livelihood. The Minangkabau, historically Sumatra's pepper-growers, are still growing pepper, and they grow coffee commercially as well. The Banda still produce 80 percent of the world's nutmeg, but the individual Bandanese rely a great deal on tourism to make a living. Many of the locals have opened scuba diving shops or offer their services as dive boat guides, since the Banda coral reefs have become a diving mecca. Bali, Lombok, Sumba, and Sumbawa are now considered great surfing islands as well.

Asmat tribesmen still carve shields and ancestor poles, but now these sculptures are collectors' items. On Papua, the Catholic missionary Crosiers help the tribe show their work, old and new, via a museum. Older pieces have head-hunting and war themes, but since head-hunting and traditional tribal warfare has been outlawed by the government, newer ones show more tranquil scenes, such as families fishing and collecting sago. Though the Asmat and their art have changed, the sale of the pieces allow the tribe to gain self-respect and money, say the Crosiers: "The art is becoming secular. Now when they sell [their work], they feel it's worthwhile. They can say, 'We are the Asmat.'"[49]

An Indonesian boy surfs in front of his village. Thousands of surfers from around the world travel to Indonesia each year to ride the archipelago's perfect waves.

93

Men of the Yali tribe prepare to perform a war dance. Some tribes like the Yali encourage tourists to visit their villages.

Other tribes engage in more mundane pursuits—islanders who live east of Bali tend plots of seaweed in the ocean, selling their crop at twenty-five cents or more a pound. Seaweed derivatives thicken such well-known products as whipping cream and wrinkle cream. The Bajau, who have converted to Islam, still fish, but their catch is earmarked for commercial sale as well as personal use.

Other tribes have managed to carve a place for themselves as tourist destinations. But in these instances, tribes themselves have become the tourist attractions—tour operators include visits to the Yali, Dani, and Asmat villages as part of the vacation package. Some observers praise this development, saying that it gives the Indonesian government a financial incentive to preserve indigenous culture. But, tribesmen often find groups of tourists to be intrusive, writes Lindsay:

> Greedy Sumatran guides arrive on Siberut with insular tour groups that are unprepared and uneducated in the ways of the Mentawaians, frequently ignoring the local customs. Locals feel cheated by gawking outsiders who leave so little of value in their wake. Though the Mentawaians welcome individual travelers, they see the growing number of tourists as an imposition.[50]

Still, for some tribes tourism may be their only hope. Supporters of the Towana tribe, which lives in the 669-square-mile Morowali Nature Reserve in Sulawesi, are looking to the tourists who visit the reserve for help in planning their future. In 2003 the tribe was looking to build a handicraft center where they could sell their native artwork and crafts. They were also looking to acquire a motorboat to transport the crafts outside the reserve and sought funds, via a website designed by a benefactor, to jumpstart their plans.

Looking to a Future

Indonesia's future remains uncertain, but how well it comes to terms with the present and the past may depend on its indigenous peoples. It may well be up to the next generation of tribesmen to preserve Indonesia's mosaic of cultures while still piloting the future of a growing nation in the modern era.

Notes

Introduction: "Our Earth and Water"

1. Ailsa Zainu'ddin, *A Short History of Indonesia*. New York: Praeger, 1970, p. 4.
2. Zainu'ddin, *A Short History of Indonesia*, pp. 3–4.

Chapter One: Rice Fields and Spices

3. Charles Corn, *The Scents of Eden, a Narrative of the Spice Islands*. New York: Kodansha America, 1998, p. 25.
4. Frank Clune, *Isles of Spice*. New York: E.P. Dutton, 1942, p. 158.
5. Tim Severin, *The Spice Islands Voyage*. New York: Carroll & Graf, 1997, p. 144.
6. Fred Bruemmer, "Sea Hunters of Lamalera," *Natural History,* October 2001, p. 58.
7. Bruemmer, "Sea Hunters of Lamalera," p. 58.
8. Quoted in Zainu'ddin, *A Short History of Indonesia*, p. 83.

Chapter Two: The Rhythms of Culture

9. Tracy Johnston, *Shooting the Boh, a Woman's Voyage Down the Wildest River in Borneo*. New York: Vintage Books, 1992, p. 37.
10. Edwin H. Gomes, "Notes on the Sea Dyaks of Borneo," National Geographic, August 1911, p. 709.
11. Jean Gelman Taylor, *Indonesia, Peoples and Histories*. New Haven, CT: Yale University Press, 2003, p. 162.
12. Malcolm S. Kirk, "The Asmat of New Guinea, Headhunters in Today's World," *National Geographic,* March 1972, p. 400.
13. Bruemmer, "Sea Hunters of Lamalera," p. 58.
14. Johnston, *Shooting the Boh*, p. 57.
15. Johnston, *Shooting the Boh*, p. 51.
16. Johnston, *Shooting the Boh*, p. 52.

Chapter Three: Going to War, Keeping the Peace

17. Zainu'ddin, *A Short History of Indonesia*, p. 53.
18. Charles Lindsay, *Mentawai Shaman, Keeper of the Rain Forest*. New York: Aperture Books, 1992, p. 77.
19. Zainu'ddin, *A Short History of Indonesia*, p. 137.
20. Quoted in Kirk, "The Asmat of New Guinea," p. 391.
21. Quoted in Zainu'ddin, *A Short History of Indonesia*, p. 78.
22. Quoted in Zainu'ddin, *A Short History of Indonesia*, p. 105.
23. Quoted in Thomas O'Neill, "Irian Jaya, Indonesia's Wild Side," *National Geographic,* February 1996, p. 28.
24. Johnston, *Shooting the Boh*, p. 56.

Chapter Four: Spirits and Ancestors

25. Corn, *The Scents of Eden,* p. 78.
26. Bruemmer, "Sea Hunters of Lamalera," p. 57.
27. Helen and Frank Schreider, "East from Bali by Seagoing Jeep to Timor," *National Geographic,* August 1962, p. 266.
28. Jean-Philippe Soulé, "The Mentawai People of Siberut, Indonesia." www.nativeplanet.org.
29. Lindsay, *Mentawai Shaman,* p. 48.
30. Quoted in Corn, *The Scents of Eden,* p. 77.
31. Helen and Frank Schreider, "Indonesia: The Young and Troubled Island Nation," *National Geographic,* May 1961, p. 622.

Chapter Five: Masters and Freedom Fighters

32. Quoted in Severin, *The Spice Islands Voyage,* p. 24.
33. D.R. Sardesai, *Southeast Asia Past and Present.* Boulder, CO: Westview Press, 1989, p. 63.
34. Zainu'ddin, *A Short History of Indonesia,* p. 107.
35. Zainu'ddin, *A Short History of Indonesia,* p. 78.
36. Zainu'ddin, *A Short History of Indonesia,* p. 145.
37. Quoted in Zainu'ddin, *A Short History of Indonesia,* p. 209.
38. Zainu'ddin, *A Short History of Indonesia,* p. 223.

Chapter Six: A People at the Crossroads

39. Severin, *The Spice Islands Voyage,* p. 25.
40. Quoted in Tracy Dahlby, "Indonesia: Living Dangerously," *National Geographic,* March 2001, p. 91.
41. Johnston, *Shooting the Boh,* p. 19.
42. Severin, *The Spice Islands Voyage,* pp. 126–27.
43. Paul Krugman, "In Praise of Cheap Labor, Bad Jobs at Bad Wages Are Better than No Jobs at All." http://web.mit.edu.
44. Johnston, *Shooting the Boh,* p. 23.
45. Melinda Liu, "Birth of a 'Messy' State," *Newsweek,* March 12, 2001, p. 40.
46. Quoted in Schreider, "Indonesia," p. 621.
47. Severin, *The Spice Islands Voyage,* p. 80.
48. Lindsay, *Mentawai Shaman,* p. 103.
49. Quoted in Lindsay, *Mentawai Shaman,* p. 113.
50. Lindsay, *Mentawai Shaman,* p. 103.

For Further Reading

Books

Julian Burger, *Gaia Book of First Peoples: A Future for the Indigenous World.* London: Gaia Books, 1990. The indigenous tribes of Indonesia are but one component of Burger's book, which takes a global view. But Burger does a good job explaining the cultural, political, economic, and human rights challenges that tribes all over the world face.

Donald W. Fryer and James C. Jackson, *Indonesia.* Boulder, CO: Westview Press, 1977. This book by Jackson and Fryer is a bit dry but contains a concise look at Indonesia's history with respectful attention paid to the indigenous peoples of the islands.

Judy Jacobs, *Indonesia, a Nation of Islands.* Minneapolis: Dillon Press, 1990. Jacobs's short and readable book explores modern Indonesian culture as well as ancient times; for example, readers will learn that Indonesians are rabid moviegoers as well as fans of traditional shadow puppet theater.

James Martin, *Komodo Dragons: Giant Lizards of Indonesia (Animals & the Environment).* Mankato, MN: Capstone Press, 1995. These very fascinating "dragons" of Indonesia get a colorful treatment in Martin's well-illustrated and informative book.

Taro McGuinn, *East Timor, Island in Turmoil.* Minneapolis: Lerner, 1998. McGuinn's book was written before East Timor achieved its independence from Indonesia in 2002. Readers who want background on these tiny and volatile island communities will get the basics from McGuinn's account.

Sylvia McNair, *Enchantment of the World, Indonesia.* Chicago: Childrens Press, 1993. Young readers will get a good introduction to Indonesia's culture, architecture, peoples, and history via this book.

Giles Milton, *Nathaniel's Nutmeg: Or, the True and Incredible Adventures of the Spice Trader Who Changed the Course of History.*

99

New York: Farrar, Straus & Giroux, 1999. Milton takes an innovative look at the spice trade by focusing on one Englishman, Nathaniel Courthope of the East India Company, who tried to hold the island of Run for England against overwhelming pressure from the Dutch over a five-year period. Advanced readers will enjoy this absorbing account, which also details the relationship between the island's indigenous peoples and the Europeans.

Mary C. Wilds, *Southeast Asia*. San Diego, CA: Lucent Books, 2003. This book puts Indonesia's indigenous tribes into the context of Southeast Asia as a whole. Contents focus on culture, religion, government, and interactions with Europeans.

Websites

Tiger Territory (www.lairweb.org). A clearinghouse for information on all species of tiger, this website also discusses the tiger range of Indonesia, which in recent years has been confined to Sumatra: The subspecies of Javan tiger has been declared extinct.

Komodo Dragon (www.nature.co). Readers who want a quick and comprehensive look at Indonesia's dragon lizards can find it at this website.

Works Consulted

Books

Nigel Barley, *Not a Hazardous Sport.* New York: Henry Holt, 1988. Barley is an anthropologist who went on a field expedition in Sulawesi during the 1980s. Barley was often dismayed by the sullying of local culture by Western influence, but he did get a close look at some surviving indigenous customs, including a Torajan funeral.

Frank Clune, *Isles of Spice.* New York: E.P. Dutton, 1942. During his travels through Indonesia, Clune assumed the kind of condescending, paternalistic, and sexist attitude that modern readers find offensive. However, he did visit the islands at a time when much of the indigenous culture, particularly on Kalimantan and Sulawesi, was mostly intact, and he shows a curious sympathy for such tribes as the Dayak and the Toraja.

Charles Corn, *The Scents of Eden, a Narrative of the Spice Islands.* New York: Kodansha America, 1998. Corn looks exclusively at the spice trade, going all the way back to early references in the Old Testament. His language is colorful and descriptive and his emphasis, as in other books, is on the European traders.

Willard A. Hanna, *Indonesian Banda.* Philadelphia: Institute for the Study of Human Resources, 1978. Hanna is mostly interested in European involvement on the Bandas, but he does discuss the farming techniques of the locals and the history of the spice trade.

Tracy Johnston, *Shooting the Boh, a Woman's Voyage Down the Wildest River in Borneo.* New York: Vintage Books, 1992. Johnston, a travel writer, traveled Kalimantan to undertake a rafting trip. But she is a good observer and includes information about the present-day living conditions of the Dayak, Kalimantan's indigenous peoples.

Charles Lindsay, *Mentawai Shaman, Keeper of the Rain Forest.* New York: Aperture Books, 1992. This well-illustrated book focuses on the Mentawai, their shamans, customs, beliefs in the afterlife, and lifestyle.

D.R. Sardesai, *Southeast Asia Past and Present.* Boulder, CO: Westview Press, 1989. The focus of Sardesai's book is more regional: The history of Indonesia is discussed along with that of other Southeast Asian countries, such as Vietnam and Thailand. However, Sardesai's sober and factual account does a good job of placing Indonesia's past in the context of a region and continent.

Tim Severin, *The Spice Islands Voyage.* New York: Carroll & Graf, 1997. Severin and his team followed the route of naturalist Alfred Russel Wallace, who toured Indonesia in a native-style craft, studying the flora and fauna of the islands and eventually coming up with a theory of evolution that predated Darwin's. Severin's book takes a more contemporary look at the flora and fauna and at the indigenous populations.

Jean Gelman Taylor, *Indonesia, Peoples and Histories.* New Haven, CT: Yale University Press, 2003. Taylor's book focuses mostly on the upper echelons of Java and Sumatra and on Indonesia's ruling families. Her book contains photographs of ancient sites and capsule histories of the spice trade, animism, and other aspects of life in Indonesia.

Ailsa Zainu'ddin, *A Short History of Indonesia.* New York: Praeger, 1970. Zainu'ddin's well-written and highly readable account offers a concise account of Indonesian history. While Zainu'ddin puts much of her emphasis on the Europeans, she does offer enough insight into the local peoples to give a flavor of precolonial Indonesia.

Periodicals

Fred Bruemmer, "Sea Hunters of Lamalera," *Natural History,* October 2001.

Tracy Dahlby, "Indonesia: Living Dangerously," *National Geographic,* March 2001.

Ray T. Elsmore, "New Guinea's Mountain and Swampland Dwellers," *National Geographic,* December 1945.

Vaudine England, "Inheriting Indonesia: The Dream That Never Was," *World Press Review,* October 2001.

Edwin H. Gomes, "Notes on the Sea Dyaks of Borneo," *National Geographic,* August 1911.

James A. Kern, "Dragon Lizards of Komodo," *National Geographic,* December 1968.

Malcolm S. Kirk, "The Asmat of New Guinea, Headhunters in Today's World," *National Geographic*, March 1972.

Melinda Liu, "Birth of a 'Messy' State," *Newsweek,* March 12, 2001.

Peter Miller, "Bali Celebrates a Festival of Faith," *National Geographic,* March 1980.

Thomas O'Neill, "Irian Jaya, Indonesia's Wild Side," *National Geographic,* February 1996.

Helen and Frank Schreider, "East from Bali by Seagoing Jeep to Timor," *National Geographic,* August 1962.

———,"Indonesia: The Young and Troubled Island Nation," *National Geographic,* May 1961.

Science, "The End for Indonesia's Lowland Forests?" May 4, 2001.

Michael Shari, "Is a Holy War Brewing in Indonesia?" *Business Week,* October 15, 2001.

George Steinmetz, "Irian Jaya's People of the Trees," *National Geographic,* February 1996.

Internet Sources

ABC, "Lateline: Balinese Cleanse Kuta Bomb Site." www.abc.net. This Australian news program published a transcript online regarding its coverage of a Balinese cleansing ceremony, conducted in honor of those killed in the Bali bombings.

CNN, "At Least 183 Dead in Bali Bombings," October 13, 2002. www.cnn.com. This CNN article contains an on-the-spot account of the bombings, which targeted international visitors and were linked to the al-Qaeda terror network.

Paul Krugman, "In Praise of Cheap Labor, Bad Jobs at Bad Wages Are Better than No Jobs at All." http://web.mit.edu. Krugman, a Princeton economist, makes a case in this online article that global trade and the globalization of American corporations helps Third World peoples more than it hurts them.

Jean-Philippe Soulé, "The Mentawai People of Siberut, Indonesia." www.nativeplanet.org. Researcher Soulé lived with the Mentawai tribe in their home territory of Siberut, recording their customs, lifestyle, and religious traditions, which remain under threat by the modern world. He details his findings on his website.

Index

Picture Credits

Cover Photo: © Bill Morris
© AFP/CORBIS, 90, 92
© Bettmann/CORBIS, 67
© Dean Conger/CORBIS, 70
© CORBIS, 78
Corel Corporation, 24, 38
© Hulton/Archive, 50, 75, 82
© Hulton-Deutsch Collection/CORBIS, 33, 48, 73
© Colin Garratt; Milepost 92 ½/CORBIS, 69
© Dustin Humphrey/A-Frame, 14, 61, 93
© Wolfgang Kaehler/CORBIS, 76
© Charles and Josette Lenars/CORBIS, 18, 58
© Bill Morris, 22, 29, 30, 36, 44, 54, 87
Brandy Noon, 11, 28
© Jim Russi, 43
© Anders Ryman/CORBIS, 60
© Albrecht G. Schaefer/CORBIS, 17, 94
SUPRI/Reuters/Landov, 85

About the Author

Mary C. Wilds has authored *Southeast Asia* and *The Shawnee,* for Lucent Books, and a series of books on black history for Avisson Press. She lives in Indiana.